Contemporary Narrative

D1428746

Library
01254 292120

Please return this book on or before the last date below

Also available from Continuum:

Adaptation in Contemporary Culture: Textual Infidelities
Edited by Rachel Carroll

The Novel: An Alternative History
Steven Moore

The Seven Basic Plots: Why We Tell Stories
Christopher Booker

Contemporary Narrative
Textual Production, Multimodality and Multiliteracies

Fiona J. Doloughan

continuum

Continuum International Publishing Group

The Tower Building   80 Maiden Lane
11 York Road   Suite 704
London SE1 7NX   New York, NY 10038

www.continuumbooks.com

© Fiona J. Doloughan 2011

British Library Cataloguing-in-Publication Data
A catalogue record for this book is available from the British Library.

ISBN: 978-1-4411-2199-8 (Hardback)
       978-1-4411-2800-3 (Paperback)

Library of Congress Cataloging-in-Publication Data
A catalog record for this book is available from the Library of Congress.

Typeset by Newgen Imaging Systems Pvt Ltd, Chennai, India
Printed and bound in India

This book is dedicated to the memory of Eugene H. Falk,
an outstanding scholar and inspirational teacher at
the University of North Carolina at Chapel Hill.

Contents

Preface

This book is the outcome of work undertaken in different disciplinary locations over a number of years. As a result, it brings to the study of contemporary narrative a cross-disciplinary perspective rooted in Translation Studies and Applied Linguistics as well as Narratology and Comparative Literature. The book aims to place contemporary narrative production in the context of social and technological developments and to point to the cultural and linguistic factors which have a bearing on the kinds of narratives produced as well as impacting on their mode of representation. Adopting a case study approach, the book illustrates, through analysis of pertinent examples, the extent to which narratives today can be seen to relate to a number of critical and creative dimensions. These dimensions are explored in the book in relation to the key concepts of *multimodality, multiliteracies* and *translation.*

If I have chosen to highlight these concepts in relation to developments in contemporary narrative, it is primarily because they seem to offer a way of accounting for developments which might otherwise appear random and unmotivated. Using insights and terminology from multimodality and employing translation as an enabling metaphor, I hope to show that individual narrative production is marked by contextual and cultural forces which shape the emergent text in particular ways. With respect to the shape and import of narrative and specifically to the question of how stories are told in the late twentieth and early twenty-first centuries, multimodality and a broad view of translation help shed light on the following perceived trends and issues:

- increasing interest in the possibilities and limitations of the visual mode for contemporary storytelling
- concern with finding a language (or languages) which adequately represent/s and 'translate/s' aspects of existence today
- renewed interest in adapting storylines across modes and media and concern with the consequences of such processes of adaptation
- the need to be able to negotiate different language and literacy practices

The book is divided into six chapters, which can be read discretely depending on reader interest. However, they are intended to speak to one another and serve cumulatively to flesh out the contentions made in relation to narrative today. These contentions relate primarily to the production of narrative but have implications for its reception. The fact, for example, that some writers are inflecting English with a variety of linguistic and cultural accents in their creation of narratives that translate cultural and linguistic difference, may well be received differently depending on the extent of a particular reader's access to and experience of other languages and cultures. Likewise, writers who draw on a variety of modalities (e.g. visual as well as verbal modes) or who experiment with genre may challenge readers of more conventional narratives. This, however, is what writers have always done: they have taken prevailing norms and conventions and transformed them into something else, something otherwise; and they have borrowed old stories, dusted them down and turned them into something new.

Acknowledgements

From its genesis to its completion, this book has depended on a number of individuals besides the author, individuals whose contribution I wish to acknowledge here. At the level of ideas which have gone into the making of this book, I wish to acknowledge in particular the influence of the work of Gunther Kress, a former colleague at the Institute of Education, University of London whose writings on social semiotics in general and multimodality in particular have been extremely productive in helping to advance my own thinking in relation to contemporary narrative.

I would also like to thank Margaret Rogers, Head of the Centre for Translation Studies at the University of Surrey, for encouraging a nascent interest in Translation and Creativity, a theme which underlies much of what I say in the book, and for pointing me in the right direction in terms of the Translation Studies literature.

In addition, I would like to acknowledge the input of my students. In developing and teaching modules in Creative Writing, I had the opportunity to test some of my ideas and get feedback on them.

At a more practical level, I wish to acknowledge the sabbatical leave granted to me by the University of Surrey to enable me to devote time to my project, and particularly thank Marion Wynne-Davies, my very supportive Head of Department, who graciously picked up extra work in my absence. For providing constructive feedback on individual chapters, my thanks go to Margaret and Marion as well as Sarah Gibson, my colleagues at Surrey, and to the initial reviewers of my sample chapter. I have no doubt that the book is better as a result of this input. Remaining inadequacies are entirely my own.

My thanks also go to Anna Fleming and Colleen Coalter at Continuum for preparing the manuscript for publication.

Last, but by no means, least, I owe a debt of gratitude to my partner, Regine.

Chapter 1

New Perspectives on Narrative

Introductory Remarks

This is a book about narrative and the ways in which it is shaped and articulated today. In the course of the book, the various forces at work in helping to construct contemporary narratives will be seen to relate to cultural, linguistic, social and technological factors and to new conceptualizations of and approaches to narrative. While the book will attempt to 'abstract away' from the specifics of individual narratives in order to highlight points of more general import, it will in the main do so in relation to discussion of particular cases chosen to reflect more general tendencies. In other words, this is not primarily a book about narrative in the abstract nor is it a theoretical discussion of conceptualizations of it. Rather, it is an attempt to situate contemporary narrative practices in relation to an explanatory and descriptive framework which appears to account for some current narrative developments. It is hoped that the case study approach will allow for a balance between analysis of a specific work or set of works and discussion of its or their relevance to the wider issues pertaining to developments in and issues relating to narrative.

Clearly, the whole question of what constitutes a narrative will have to be addressed in relation to current thinking and a justification given for the perspective adopted in this book. Broadly speaking, within the context of narrative production, the focus will be on writing as cognitive and affective intervention in the storehouse of the narrative past in the light of present contingencies and/or future considerations. This intervention will involve transformation of existing textual resources in an attempt to create something new or different. However, as will become apparent, the book does not restrict itself to written narratives but is also concerned with the ways in which narratives presented in one mode (e.g. the visual or the verbal) or medium (e.g. in print or on screen) are or can be transposed or 'translated' across modes and media. Indeed, the notion of translation will function as an enabling metaphor in attempts to understand the processes involved in the transfer and transformation of substance and/or ideas from one mode or medium to another.

This position may appear to be at odds with the idea that content is always formed and therefore in an absolute sense inextricably bound up with the manner in which its substance is shaped and the material presented. While not wishing to deny the importance of the manner in which ideas are presented and entities projected, as will become apparent, the focus of interest will lie in the possibilities for narrative transmission of storylines across modes and media and in the extent to which narratives adapt to new sets of circumstances. Furthermore, it will be argued that it is precisely the availability and relative accessibility of different modes and media in contemporary society that paves the way for the production of new kinds of narrative.

In the context of a view that the availability of and access to linguistic, cultural and technological resources is a pre-condition for the production of (new) narratives, the role of language/s will be seen to be important. One of the more controversial contentions of the book, perhaps, from an Anglo-American perspective, is that bilingualism/multilingualism has the potential to enhance or enrich narrative production. Such a contention depends on a particular view of the relationship of language and culture and on a notion of creativity, which sees language/s as a resource for meaning-making. In a world where bilingualism/multilingualism is the norm rather than the exception and where English has become a kind of lingua franca, it is useful to examine the implications of this situation for contemporary narrative.

It would be impossible for a single book on narrative to do justice to all its various dimensions in relation to both theory and practice; nor would it necessarily be useful to do so, such is the scope of conceptualizations of and approaches to narrative; the range of methodological issues; and the diversity of narrative practices. However, any book on narrative, including the present one, must situate its perspective within the frame of existing work, indicating and justifying its stance. In the course of this introductory chapter, I shall attempt to position my ideas on narrative in relation to previous and current work in the field of Narrative Studies or Narratology and to make connections, where relevant, to work being carried out in other areas such as Translation Studies and Creative Writing. This is because the present work is, first and foremost, the outcome of interdisciplinary studies and the perspectives taken can be traced back to work in Comparative Literature and Applied Linguistics as well as Social Semiotics.

There is always a danger with such interdisciplinary work that in attempting to speak to all, it speaks to none. My hope is that in bringing together insights from a variety of disciplinary domains and applying them to particular texts, the unfolding argument about the forces shaping narrative production today in relation to its contemporary configurations will begin to gather momentum and assume some weight in the light of the evidence produced. There will be no definitive answers to what are by their very nature open and interdependent questions, the answers to which are likely to shift over time in response to the production of new texts, some of which will challenge neat theoretical definitions: What do we mean by narrative? To what extent has it changed over time, and why? What is the significance of narrative today? How is narrative produced and how does it function? If it is likely that narrative continues to exist, what form/s might it take? However, if this book is to do the job that it sets out to do, then by the end the reader should have a sense of the importance and cultural significance of narrative; should understand better how narratives are produced and constructed; and be aware of the factors currently impacting upon the 'shape' and texture of narratives today. On the assumption that a better understanding of the construction of narrative texts affords the opportunity for enhanced production as well as enriched reception, the book also aspires to be a kind of handbook for creative writers. For, as will be shown in what follows, for many writers, 'inspiration' and the drive to produce something new stems from an encounter with and desire to respond to key texts from the past.

Some Key Assumptions and Key Terms

In examining what appear to be the forces shaping contemporary narrative and presenting a snapshot of aspects of narrative today, I am working with a number of assumptions and under the umbrella of a set of contestable notions concerning narrative and its design principles. Let me start by making these assumptions, notions and principles explicit, before going on to define, at least provisionally, some of the key terms which underpin my ideas. I shall then relate them to my principal arguments and to some of the main trends in recent and current work on narrative.

As someone who spent a great deal of time in the 1980s working on concepts of Realism in the French and English nineteenth- and early twentieth-century novel from a comparative and theoretical perspective using the work of Genette in *Discours du récit (Narrative Discourse)* as a methodological tool, I tend to share a post-structuralist anxiety around the imposition of 'fixed' categories on texts, preferring in the main more dynamic approaches to text construction and interpretation. The dangers of reification in the process of applying analytical categories to novels with a view to uncovering their supposed structural and thematic properties are real and not to be underestimated. At the same time, however, in the absence of any method of analysis and/or theoretical or critical framework, one runs the risk of raising potentially impressionistic insights to the status of general laws. I shall therefore be working within the context of a broad narratological framework tempered with insights from critical theory, social semiotics and critical linguistics.

My borrowing and, in some cases, adapting of concepts from neighbouring disciplines is motivated by an attempt to bring relevant insights into my own field of study. Thus, for example, the concept of multimodality, developed by social semioticians such as Kress and van Leeuwen (see, for example, Kress and van Leeuwen, 2001) will inform discussion of the tendency of narratives today to avail themselves of cinematographic, visual and spatial resources in interesting and challenging ways. By multimodality, I mean the use of more than one mode in the construction of a textual entity. While classical narratology was no stranger to analyses of the visual as well as the verbal (see, for example, Barthes' *Mythologies*), developments in understanding of the ways in which different modes interact and of the ability of designers of text, including narrative texts, to compose a multimodal ensemble according to their interests, have led to the possibility of greater awareness of the influence of the choice of mode on textual construction and apperception. That insights from multimodality are of relevance to narrative theory and practice is reflected in the recent publication of *New Perspectives on Narrative and Multimodality*, an edited volume (Page, 2010) reviewing the overlapping domains of multimodality and approaches to narrative concerned to account for its evolution and current status.

This leads me to another point in relation to the assumptions operating here. While not excluding the play of the unconscious in textual production, my assumption will be that for the most part writers and designers of text try to achieve particular aims and effects using the resources at their disposal (cf. Kress's 2003 concept of the motivated sign). Some of the writers represented in this volume (e.g. Woolf, Winterson) provide ample evidence of this in terms of their sometimes self-conscious but always motivated attempts to realize a particular vision and/or achieve certain stylistic effects in their work through, for example, the use of specific narrative techniques.

This is not to suggest that all readers construct the same version or have the same vision of a text. As Iser (1978) has shown, all texts have gaps or points of indeterminacy, which readers are required to fill in. Depending on what they bring to the text as well as on their horizon of expectations, they are likely to construct or 'colour in' what they read differently. However, neither does textual comprehension proceed arbitrarily and indiscriminately but is triggered and cued by the marks and sequences on the page and constituted by social subjects on the basis of cultural and experiential scripts (Herman, 2002). Thus, the view of narrative production espoused here will see it as a series of dynamic interactions and interventions on the part of both reader and writer.

From the perspective of the reader, this involves constructing a mental model of the (fictional) world on the basis of an interpretation of the textual signifiers and responding to the virtual universe thus created at any one or all of the following levels: social, ethical, philosophical, political and aesthetic. From the writer's perspective, the twin notions of transformation and translation will be seen to be important in the creation of any kind of text, including those characterized as narrative texts. The writer will principally be viewed as a careful and responsive reader of text with a capacity to translate the potential of one text into another 'new' text. Such a view is not intended to undermine evidence of creativity on the part of writers but rather to frame this 'newness' in relation to what is or has been and to see language itself as a source of creativity (cf. notions of creative construction).

Many of the ideas articulated here are not new in the sense that they stem from and build upon the work of other theorists, critics and analysts. What is new is the bringing together of ideas and insights from different disciplinary areas to show their relevance to the particular object of study. For in looking at and trying to make sense of the ways in which narrative has developed/is developing, reliance on one field or set of interests is likely to reproduce the orthodoxies current in that field. By drawing on relevant insights from across disciplinary domains and a repertoire of sometimes competing and conflicting discourses, I hope to approach narrative from a considered if somewhat eclectic point of view.

The overarching concepts which underpin my perspective relate to notions of textual transformation and translation; and to ideas about textual construction which see it as dependent on the availability of and access to resources. By textual transformation, I mean to point to the notion that rather than creating or generating text in a vacuum, writers, consciously or otherwise, absorb and reply to other texts, thereby giving voice to what they have read, imagined and experienced in a new text that incorporates aspects of past production and evidences traces of the appropriation of the language of others (Kristeva, 1986, p. 39). In speaking of translation, I wish to foreground the notion that 'original' production is dependent on knowledge of or a degree of familiarity with prior, 'source' texts, which have left their mark on the writer as reader-interpreter and which find their way into their rendering of the new text. Clearly, this is not translation in the sense in which we might understand a writer, such as Baudelaire, to translate a text, such as one by Poe, from American-English into French. However, what I wish to show in the course of the book is that as a metaphor for text production, the concept of translation works remarkably well and permits interrogation of taken-for-granted notions about creativity. It helps shed light on the complex reader–writer interactions and interventions that take place in any reworking or 'translating' of text, whether that be from one language to another, from one mode to another or from one medium to another.

By resources I mean to refer to the kinds of knowledge, skills and instruments to which one has access. These resources are multiple and interdependent: linguistic (including grammatical and lexical resources); cultural (including knowledge of the literary system and generic conventions); social (including knowledge of the ways in which the literary system fits into the general social and political economy); technological (including the ability to realize one's vision or objectives through use of available technologies and understanding of their capabilities). From this perspective, knowledge of and access to a variety of cultures and languages is potentially beneficial and enriching in constructing a textual universe, since it allows for the possibility of structural innovation and greater semantic scope, if not depth, through selecting and combining materials and resources from across cultures.

The other terms which require some initial definition are the following: text, genre, narrative, story, discourse, mode and medium. Text refers to a cultural artefact composed or constructed by an individual or group of individuals. This cultural artefact can be made of words and/or images and is designed to communicate a message and/or tell a story. There are different kinds of text, for example narrative texts and argumentative or persuasive texts. These different kinds of text have different, conventionalized purposes. A narrative, for example, aims to tell a story, whereas an argumentative text is more concerned with putting and defending a thesis. This is not to suggest that stories may not also reflect particular positions or take a particular stance. Conversely, argumentative texts can use narrative means to advance an argument.

With respect to narrative terminology, a distinction is often drawn between 'story' and 'discourse', where the former means to refer to the linear sequence of events articulated in the narrative text, while discourse refers to the manner in which the storyline is articulated and is concerned with the implications of the choice of words for the kinds of meanings made. The basis for such a distinction is the contention that what happens in a story can be 'extracted' from the storyline and retold in other words. This distinction, while important in classical narratology, has come under attack by post-structuralists for whom it is based on a dualistic mode of thought and pre-supposes a 'pure' form of narrative unadulterated by the language in which it is articulated. As already indicated, while content is always formed and we can speak of 'formed content' to indicate the inseparability, in absolute terms, of form and content, it nevertheless seems legitimate to hold such a distinction in mind when looking at the ways in which the same 'story' can be differently realized and adapted across texts and across modes and media. Failure to accept this analytic distinction would make it difficult to account for different versions of a story (e.g. Faust; Don Quixote) and its transposition and transformation from one mode and/or medium to another.

The terms 'mode' and 'medium' refer to the manner and the means by which textual material is presented and conducted. For example, a story, such as the death of Christ, may be presented pictorially or it may be related verbally. In the first case, the story, relayed visually, may be viewed on the walls of a chapel or be reproduced on the page or on the screen. In the second case, the story told orally or 'read out' from a biblical source may be transmitted through the air or airwaves and captured on tape or it may be rendered in written form in a book or pamphlet. Where it can get confusing is in deciding whether language is mode or medium or both. We often talk about language as a medium of communication, for example, in the sense of one of many means whereby communication can be effected. Language can be delivered in the spoken mode or the written mode and transmitted via audio or video, for example; language in the written mode can be presented in print or on screen, two different media which, as we will see, have the capacity to impact upon the organization and configuration of the written text, particularly in cases where many modes are employed to deliver the message, communicate ideas or construct a narrative.

Before turning to an overview of the literature on narrative and sketching out the main areas of contention in narrative theory and accounts of narrative practice, let me set out the principal concerns and key ideas of the book.

- It attributes recent developments in narrative to a number of factors, including technological advances and the affordances of the new media; and to increasing multilingualism and multiculturalism.
- It inscribes a multidimensional view of text and sees all texts, including narrative texts, as potentially multimodal.
- It sees writers as skilful and responsive readers of text who create new texts from imaginative reworkings and creative transformations of previous texts.
- As material artefacts produced by human subjects, it suggests that the production of new narratives depends on access to a range of linguistic, cultural, social and technological resources.

Conceptualizations of and Approaches to Narrative

As David Herman (2007) makes clear in his introduction to *The Cambridge Companion to Narrative*, approaches to narrative can essentially be divided into the classical and the post-classical (p. 12). Briefly, and without going into the whole history of narrative, which is not the subject of this book, by classical approaches he means to refer to the work done by structuralist narratologists, such as Genette (termed 'the arch-geometrician of narrative' by Gibson, 2000, p. 155) and the early Mieke Bal, in the wake of attempts by some of the Russian Formalists, such as Propp, to characterize and categorize the principal functions of narrative in relation to its perceived structural and thematic properties. With respect to post-classical approaches, he is aiming to point to the influence on narratology of insights from a whole range of areas 'from gender theory and philosophical ethics, to (socio)linguistics, philosophy of language, and cognitive science, to comparative media studies and critical theory' (Herman, 2007, p. 12).

Herman himself, with his dual background in English Literature and Cognitive Linguistics, has been responsible for enriching classical approaches to narrative through a focus on the cues which aim to trigger the cognitive construction of a storyworld, or mental model of a (fictional) world in which participants act and events take place in space and time, by readers responding to the design of the narrative in question at both a local and a global level, what Herman (2002) refers to as narrative micro- and macro-designs. In other words, Herman has shifted the terrain towards a more dynamic model of narrative text construction insofar as he is interested in the interface between writer, as producer of written text, and reader, as consumer/recipient of that text; and in the textual and cognitive processes which might inform the reader's grasp of a particular kind of narrative. In this sense, the design of the narrative text serves as a kind of roadmap for the reader and guides his/her construction and experience of the storyworld.

That there have been developments in the ways in which narrative theory and analysis is approached since the days of Russian Formalism and Structuralism is echoed by de Lauretis (2000) who claims that 'narrative theory is no longer or not primarily intent on establishing a logic, a grammar, or a formal rhetoric of narrative; what it seeks to understand is the nature of the structuring and destructuring, even destructive, processes at work in textual and semiotic production' (p. 206). The focus on process rather than simply on product, indeed the idea of dialogue between the two might be seen as characteristic of more recent, or what Gibson (2000, p. 156) terms, revisionist, approaches to narrative which seek to move away from static structural models towards 'the dynamics of text as actualized in the reading process' (Brooks, 2000, p. 152). However, for Gibson (2000, p. 154), American narratology, in particular, appears to be haunted by a 'geometrics', rather than an 'energetics', of narrative. He sees the work of Ryan, for instance, as returning to 'the assumption that there are basic, cognitive elements to all narratives' and to the 'supposed purity, clarity, uniformity and universality of narrative space (p. 157)'.

Ryan's recent work (2007) has produced a fuzzy-set definition of narrative which tries to avoid strict boundaries and mutually exclusive binary terms. It moves away from the idea that all narratives either have or have not certain properties in favour of 'a scalar conception of narrative' (p. 28), allowing 'variable degrees of membership' as one moves from 'the marginal cases to the prototypes' (p. 28). She speaks of 'degree of narrativity' (p. 30) and attempts to link her 'conditions of narrativity' (p. 28) organized along four different dimensions – the spatial; the temporal; the mental; and the formal and pragmatic (p. 29) – to particular genres. For Ryan, what is important in defining narrative is that it should 'work for different media [. . .] and it should not privilege literary forms' (p. 26). Her insistence on finding a way to theorize narrative that allows for its application across modes and media is important in permitting a broad rather than a narrow view of narrative. For this reason, she privileges the term 'story' in relation to her proposed view that 'narrative is a discourse that conveys a story' (p. 26), indicating that 'story' as a mental representation 'is not tied to any particular medium, and [. . .] is independent of the distinction between fiction and non-fiction' (p. 26).

I have already flagged up the issue of terminology in Narrative Studies. It is, however, not just a question of terminological and definitional differences but a case of sometimes competing and conflicting views of narrative itself. To say that there are a number of faultlines in Narrative Studies is perhaps to overstate the case. However, broadly speaking, debates in and about narrative can be seen to relate to the following sets of (interlinking) parameters, each of which I shall take in turn, after summarizing the issues involved:

Definitions of narrative. Discussion centres on the extent to which components and characteristics of a narrative text can be distinguished and identified and indeed on the question of whether such attempts to categorize texts are feasible, useful or even desirable.

The scope and significance of narrative. This relates to a complex of issues revolving around questions of the ubiquity (or otherwise) of narrative and the extent to which narrative is considered a particular mode of thought or one of a number of text types.

The degree of universality or relativity of narrative. This relates to the extent to which it is possible to enumerate a determinate set of narrative constituents and narrative forms which are available for use and are considered meaningful across cultures.

Narrative design, construction and reception. What is at issue here is the question of the extent to which principles governing the design of a narrative or set of narratives may be identified and generalized and of the degree of alignment between the articulation of the work (as designed) and its apperception and construction by a reader or group of readers.

The relative importance of the spatial and the temporal in narrative. The issue here relates to definitions of narrative and what are considered to be its core characteristics. Minimal definitions of narrative often characterize it as a sequence of (causally connected) events experienced (by a subject) in and through time. The privileging of the temporal over the spatial can be challenged in the light of the possibilities for narrative construction afforded by the new technologies.

The relationship between narrative and genre. Like narrative, the term genre is not always transparent and can be used to refer to different conceptualizations of aspects of text. However, the main issue in respect of narrative and genre is the question of whether narrative is simply one of a number of genres (e.g. in contradistinction to argument) or whether narrative is more like a fundamental mode of human thought which can be realized across a range of genres using different modes and media (cf. political narratives, media narratives, film narratives).

The relationship between narrative and gender. In conceptualizations of narrative which see it as following a particular kind of trajectory or arc, broadly speaking as a goal-oriented, more or less linear process undertaken by an actant or subject in search of an object, the question arises of whether such a trajectory or arc can be aligned with issues of gender. Allied to this, is the question of the possibility of a kind of writing which is distinctly female (cf. écriture féminine).

The relationship between the history of narrative and the history of the novel. Depending on one's conceptualization of narrative, this relates to the question of whether narrative representation pre-dates or is co-extensive with the history of the novel. Given the focus of many classical narratologists on literary narratives, a number of questions arise regarding the possible historical and cultural specificity of narrative forms and subjects; the 'difference/s', if any, between 'fictional' and other kinds of narrative representations; and the possibility of narrative realization across modes and media.

Definitions of Narrative

Underpinning definitions of narrative is a view that narratives can be distinguished from non-narratives and that they evidence certain characteristic traits which cause them to be recognized as such by readers. The logic of the premise is undeniable but in practice determining whether a stretch of text constitutes a narrative or not can be problematic and relate to wider issues of context, both context of situation and cultural context, as well as to the perceived purpose of the text in question. Notwithstanding these difficulties, there is, in theory, a measure of agreement among those who see narrative as subject to description. In the main, these features include reference to sequencing and notions of causality in relation to the depiction of events, sets of circumstances and behaviours on the part of participants or actants.

For example, Toolan's (2001) definition of narrative, from a critical linguistic perspective, cites the following traits as constitutive of narrative:

> A narrative is a perceived sequence of non-randomly connected events, typically involving, as the experiencing agonist, humans or quasi-humans, or other sentient beings, from whose experience we humans can 'learn'. (Toolan, 2001, p. 8)

Toolan's definition reflects the fact that for something to be a narrative, it has to be perceived by a reader or listener as such; in this sense, rather than a given, it is a construct activated by the reader or listener on the basis of his/her prior experience of narratives. The other interesting aspect of narrative picked up by Toolan relates to that of human experience. He suggests that one of the functions of narrative is to instruct insofar as we can 'learn' from it through our encounters with and responses to the thoughts and actions of the characters who occupy the virtual world we have constructed. Just what we can learn, he doesn't specify but we might assume it to include knowledge of the motivations which drive the characters we have come to know in the particular fictional universe or storyworld and by extension of ourselves as humans and of the world around us, depending on the nature of the narrative. The point is that for Toolan, narrative has a function which relates to the type and extent of narrative progression. In short, narrative sets in train a motivated chain of events perceived as such by the reader/listener.

The perceived purposefulness of narrative, its rootedness in time, and its joint construction by writer and reader of a world populated by sentient beings is also reflected in Ryan's (2007, pp. 29–30) eight conditions for narrative. However, she acknowledges that not all conditions need to be met by all narratives and that different types of narrative text may well display a different conjunction of conditions. Importantly, she suggests that rather than being intrinsic to the text, some conditions, such as condition 8 – The story must communicate something meaningful to the audience – reflect 'a dimension relative to the context and to the interests of the participants' (p. 30). This is an acknowledgement of the role that context can play in situating texts and in ascribing particular significance to them.

As a social semiotician, Ryan is concerned with how meanings are constructed and how signs are read and decoded by individual readers and groups of readers. From her perspective, narrative is 'less a culturally recognized category [. . .] than an analytical concept designed by narratologists' (p. 32) whose aim is 'to delimit the object of their discipline, to isolate the features relevant to their inquiry, and to stem the recent inflation of the term narrative' (p. 33). She is here alluding to the multiplication of contexts in which the term narrative is used and to the perceived loss of clarity in relation to what might be meant by the term narrative. The danger is that if everything qualifies as narrative, we no longer have a sense of its material and cultural specificity. However, it can be argued that the widening net cast by narrative across disciplines and domains is reflective not of lack of clarity or evidence of inflation but of recognition of the extent to which 'storytelling' is part and parcel of our way of apprehending and articulating our experience of (aspects of) reality. At this level narrative is fundamental to human experience. In an effort to understand the world around us and our experience of it, we 'story' aspects of our existence and pass on knowledge and insights from one generation to the next.

For as Cobley (2001, p. 2) reminds us: 'Wherever there are humans there appear to be stories', stories about history and about life history; stories about psyches; stories told in books and newspapers; stories told on radio, television and the big screen. However, as he goes on to point out, narrative and story are not the same thing: ' "narrative" [is] a communicative relation which is often conflated with straightforward understanding of what a story is' (pp. 2–3). Rather, 'narrative is a particular form of representation implementing signs' and 'is necessarily bound up with sequence, space and time' (p. 3). Moreover, narrative is 'part of the general process of *representation* which takes place in human discourse' (p. 3; italics in original).

In some ways, such a definition poses as many questions as it appears to answer. It distinguishes 'story' and 'narrative' to the extent that narrative is seen as a re-presentation of the events of a story configured in space and time through discourse, where discourse is understood to refer to the verbal patternings and choice of lexis employed to render the narrative. Yet, in characterizing narrative as part of the general process of representation, Cobley shifts discussion away from the possible particularities of narrative towards the wider question of how representation of human actions and behaviours is effected in language, and/or through communication systems more generally, and seeks to understand what is involved in the process of signification, of which signification by narrative means is presumably only a part.

This brings me to a further point: definitions of narrative are not neutral but tend to reflect or be embedded within particular conceptualizations of and approaches to narrative. It is scarcely surprising that understandings of and ways of talking about narrative differ across domains (e.g. communication and media; literary and cultural studies) given the different histories and methodological preferences of these areas as well as their differing goals and objects of enquiry. It is important, then, to try to situate definitions of and approaches to narrative in relation to disciplinary, epistemological and methodological preferences.

Thus, Herman's view of narrative 'as a discourse genre and a cognitive style, as well as a resource for writing' (Herman, 2002, p. 1) can be seen to reflect his dual interests in literature and cognitive linguistics. As Herman (2002, p. 5) himself makes clear, his thesis is that 'both language theory and narrative theory can be viewed as resources for – or modular components of – cognitive science'. His articulation of the dimensions of narrative both in relation to its production and comprehension/reception must be seen in the light of his declared interest in modes of cognition. What is of particular interest from my perspective in Herman's work is his acknowledgement of the 'interface between narrative and cognition' (p. 5), and his systematic attempts to uncover the processes by which readers experience and are able to construct (an account of) a virtual world. In linking aspects of the micro-design of the narrative text (e.g. the functional roles assigned to participants and their grammatical and lexical realization) to aspects of the macro-design (e.g. the ways in which readers are induced to follow events and happenings from a particular perspective), he manages to provide an interface between the work done by the writer in choosing particular sets of relations and presenting and ordering them in specific ways, and that done by the reader in comprehending a narrative and constructing a storyworld.

Another aspect of Herman's work which is consonant with the perspective adopted here is his interest in the spatial, and not just the temporal properties of narrative. Of the definitions we have examined thus far, most have stressed the (motivated) sequencing of events in time. While clearly time plays an important role in narrative, for both reader and writer, in privileging the temporal, it is all too easy to forget or sideline the spatial dimension of narrative text – indeed of any text. By spatial dimension, I mean to refer not only to the imagined world reconstructed in time and space by the reader on the basis of verbal cues (Herman, 2002) but also to a writer's decision to set out the story in 'blocks' which connect or cohere at the level of language rather than at the level of plot. Here the role of metaphor and of image becomes important in making sense of (the chain of) events recounted at the level of story.

This posits a view of text, including narrative text, as being potentially polyphonic and multimodal and of the possibility of different types of inter-action between and among the various 'layers' of the work (see, for example, Falk's 1981 articulation, following Ingarden, of the literary work of art as composed of four interacting layers). As we will see, Modernist works already activated the spatial potentials of text, a trend which is being developed today as a consequence of extended understandings of what narrative is and/or entails and as a result of the affordances of the new media which actualize spatial extension through the use of links and hyperlinks.

The Scope and Significance of Narrative

In December 2004, an international conference at the University of Helsinki examined the apparent ubiquity of narrative under the banner, 'The Travelling Concept of Narrative'. The conference brought together scholars from a variety of disciplines including Linguistics, Social Anthropology, Literary Studies, Cultural Studies, History, Sociology and Film Studies to review the place of narrative in the contemporary academy and to examine the question of the usefulness of a seemingly dispersed and multidisciplinary concept. From its roots in Literature and the Humanities, narrative as a theoretical enterprise and critical and methodological tool has spread to the Social Sciences and indeed to areas such as Medicine (cf. the current focus on illness narratives) and Management Studies.

For some (e.g. Rimmon-Kenan), there is a danger in such diversity of terminological confusion and in seeking consensus at a level of generality at the expense of sometimes fruitful disciplinary disagreements. For others, such as Mieke Bal, disciplinary cross-fertilization can be useful in pointing to areas of narrative theory and practice requiring re-examination. For example, in the age of what she termed 'migratory aesthetics', she saw it as important to give greater weight to the 'where' rather than the 'who' in narrative by replacing the (problematic) concept of 'voice' with the concept of 'path', that is to focus on the trajectories taken by the participants in the narrative and on their locations (central or marginal) relative to a represented social world.

The various entries in the *Routledge Encyclopedia of Narrative Theory* by Martin Kreiswirth which treat the 'Narrative Turn in the Humanities' address the question of narrative's rise and apparent ubiquity.

> By appearing practically everywhere and assuming an enormous range of discursive functions, narrative cannot help but flaunt its inherent multi- or trans-disciplinarity; and this situation generates both its explanatory appeal and its disciplinary and definitional problems, both inside and outside the humanities and, indeed, inside and outside the walls of academia itself. (Kreiswirth, 2008, p. 378)

Kreiswirth goes on to suggest that the humanities need to re-examine narrative in the light of its migration to other disciplinary areas and to learn from its treatment elsewhere, for example as a storied form of knowledge. Indeed he argues that a consequence of this migration has been an attempt to focus on trans-disciplinary aspects of narrative which enable new understandings of narrative to develop.

> Hence narrative theory after the narrative turn must confront fictive and non-fictive narratives [. . .] in tandem, touching as much as possible on the range of narrative forms and the various media through which they are distributed. (Kreiswirth, 2008, p. 382)

What Kreiswirth is pointing to is current interest in what happens when stories travel across modes and media, how they are 'told' or conveyed in the new context and how different modes and media interact to produce particular narrative effects.

This is where theories and insights from other areas, such as multimodality and notions of translation come into play and where ideas stemming from one area can fruitfully be transposed and adapted to issues arising in a neighbouring area. To put it differently, there is evidence to suggest that Narrative Studies is at a kind of crossroads and must decide how to proceed. A confluence of cultural and technological factors, as well as acknowledgement of theoretical gaps and methodological inadequacies, has led to a position where understandings of narrative; where and how it operates; and the possibilities for the emergence of new forms, social locations and narrative practices require a revisiting and reformulation of its premises and guiding principles.

Such a reconfiguring of narrative theory and analysis is already taking place in relation to narrative and multimodality (see contributions in Page, 2010). As Page (2010, p. 4) notes in her introduction:

> Multimodality requires us to fundamentally rethink the position of verbal resources within semiotic configurations (here specifically within narrative theory) and to ask *what* the narrative system would look like if we examine other modes with equal priority.

This call to rethink narrative in terms of its multidimensional potential, a potential which may be differently realized across modes and media is a timely one, given the changing cultural and technological world in which we operate today and the consequent changes to the communicational landscape. While language continues to be extremely important in human interaction and narratives continue to be conveyed through words, language is not the sole purveyor of messages, stories, or more generally acts of communication. Increasingly, writers and readers are resorting to multiple means of communication and are availing themselves of a variety of tools, techniques, modes and media for the construction of narrative texts. Understanding and accounting for these changes as well as being able to articulate their effects on text design, production and reception requires drawing on whatever theories appear to offer an explanatory or descriptive framework. Multimodality is one such area; translation, in a broad sense, is another.

Within Translation Studies, as within Narrative as an object of study, the parameters of enquiry have been widening. Relatively new areas of study, such as Audio description, whereby blind or partially sighted individuals are given access to artefacts, images, movements and/or dramatic actions through audio descriptive narratives, have foregrounded issues relating to intersemiotic translation and what happens when one mode (e.g. the visual) is replaced or rendered by another (e.g. the verbal). In this sense, Translation Studies has been grappling with issues more commonly associated perhaps with literary and cultural studies, and film insofar as the possibilities and constraints of different modes and media are seen to be relevant to audio describers in museum, theatre, dance and film contexts. Processes of selection (i.e. what to include and what to exclude) and of narrative presentation (i.e. how to sequence actions and events as well as how to present them in terms of 'perspective' or 'point of view') become part and parcel of the considerations that the audio describer needs to keep in mind, not to mention the very real technical and temporal constraints (fitting the audio description into the pauses between scenes or stretches of dialogue in the cinema or theatre, for example).

In addition, increased interest in the creative aspects of translation as a mode (see Bassnett and Bush, 2006; and Loffredo and Perteghella, 2007) and of the role of the reader in co-constructing the (translated) text has brought the problematics and dynamics of translation closer to those of the creative writer. This overlapping terrain will be further explored in subsequent chapters and will be of particular interest in Chapter 5, 'Cultural Transformations of Narrative', which will explore the dynamics of narrative text production in relation to notions of creativity.

The Degree of Universality or Relativity of Narrative

Insofar as telling stories appears to be a universal activity regardless of language or culture, we can say that there appears to be a human propensity for narrative.

The question arises, however, of the universality or relativity of the ways in which human experience is storied and understood as well as of the type of interface between the substance, material properties or resources of narrative and its formal or thematic realization, on the assumption that story and discourse can be separated.

I have already touched on this issue in relation to discussion of the basis of definitions of narrative and the question of whether it is possible to identify basic narrative constituents or construct narrative typologies that hold regardless of culture or context. This is clearly what early formalist and structuralist pioneers of narrative were trying to do. However, such a decontextualized or highly abstracted view of narrative has been challenged on a number of grounds from various quarters.

First, notions of text immanence, that is that properties or qualities reside in or within a text, have been challenged by the view that readings of and responses to texts, including narrative texts, are constructed and projected by a reader, albeit on the basis of textual cues or marks on the page inscribed by the writer. Given the skeletal or schematic nature of any text, with its points of indeterminacy (Iser, 1978), readers are obliged to 'fill in' the gaps in line with textual cues. However, not all readers are likely to concretize a text in the same way, given differences in their experience, expectations and preferences. Cultures of reading and modes of interpretation are seen to impact upon our experience of and interaction with a text.

As a consequence of this, there has been recognition of narrative as a kind of learnt behaviour involving sets of expectations and the manipulation of generic conventions on the part of both reader and writer. As we will see, the prevalence and distribution of particular genres and narrative conventions is not fixed or static. Rather knowledge of differences in reader expectations and in the deployment of particular generic conventions can lead to a writer's ability to generate new forms or to combine existing narrative forms in interesting ways – see, for example, Chapter 4 on 'Intercultural Translation'.

Moreover, notwithstanding the view that narrative is a mode of human cognition (Herman, 2002) or 'a basic human strategy for coming to terms with time, process, and change' (Herman, 2007, p. 3), more historicist views of narrative would wish to show it to be an ideologically infused and historically and culturally grounded phenomenon whose trajectory can be seen to have much in common with the rise of the novel and the growth of the mercantile and middle classes in Western Europe. From this perspective, narrative is a mode of representation which relates to and comments on aspects of the social reality it is seen to depict and thus is always in dialogue with the discourses of the historical moment and their traces, which persist in and perhaps conflict with the discourses dominant in the present.

Additionally, narrative can be seen to serve the interests of particular groups or types of individuals within society and to set out an agenda or inscribe particular sets of values. The *Bildungsroman* would be an example of a type of narrative text which attempted to instruct its readership by showing the passage of a protagonist from uninitiated, possibly naïve and idealistic youth to more experienced, and potentially disillusioned adulthood, as s/he negotiates the challenges of living in and contributing to society. In this respect, narrative can be seen to have conservative rather than radical tendencies, though of course many novelists have attempted to bring about a change in society through their depiction of states of affairs, behaviours and practices, which are questioned or negatively evaluated in their work. We can think of Dickens' oeuvre, for example, as serving to highlight social injustices and moral dilemmas in the Victorian age or the work of contemporary writers, such as Sarah Waters, as attempting to rewrite narrative history by presenting and bringing to life predominantly lesbian characters within her (research-led) presentation of a fictional world.

This takes me to another point: as a form of storied knowledge, narrative can be seen to have an important place across and within cultures. However, it does not follow that all cultures value the same types of knowledge nor that they put equal store on the same modes of knowledge transmission. In Western society, scientific modes of thought and knowledge transmission have tended to be privileged at the expense of narrative modes, which are often viewed as more anecdotal, subjective and impressionistic, and less analytic and rigorous than more empiric, fact-based and data-driven modes of enquiry. However, as post-structuralist thinkers have pointed out, science itself is subject to a culture of narrativity and to the use of rhetorical tropes (cf. notions of 'objectivity' and 'subjectivity'; 'fact' and 'fiction'). Insofar as science has been talked about and written about in particular ways, it too constitutes a kind of grand narrative (cf. Lyotard, 1984).

One of the threads explored in what follows is the relationship of narrative and culture with the prospect of using ideas about narrative and narrative expectations as resources for writing. For writers who have access to more than one culture, there is the possibility of employing knowledge of different cultural norms to good narrative effect by, for example, thematizing cultural difference and/or 'translating' one culture for the benefit of another. This will be explored in Chapter 4 in relation to the intercultural narrative.

Narrative Design, Construction and Reception

As already indicated, one of the shifts that has taken place in Narrative Studies is a move from narrative production to narrative reception. However, this is not an either/or situation, as we have seen in relation to Herman's efforts to provide an interface position between the principles governing text design at micro- and macro-levels and the efforts undertaken by readers to comprehend a narrative text and construct a storyworld on the basis of the textual cues presented to them. Clearly, such a shift has been motivated partly by reader-response theory and by theories of language and communication that point to the skeletal nature of text and to the dynamics of textual processing as well as to the interactive nature of reading and writing.

The position taken here, following Kress (2000), will construct writers as designers of text who use the resources (linguistic, cultural, technological) at their disposal in motivated ways to achieve particular goals and effects. Such a view aims to return some agency to writers as producers of text and sees them as making choices in the presentation of the worlds they project and help to construct. This is not to negate or deny the role of the reader in bringing a textual world to life by interacting with it and, in a sense, co-constructing it. However, it is to acknowledge that the writer has an important role in constraining, if not determining, the ways in which readers react.

Clearly, there are other factors at work in text design, construction and reception. One of the arguments presented here is that the design of narratives today is enabled by the various modes and media available for its production such that it is not sustainable to treat only narratives produced verbally or graphically. As Herman points out, we must also address the issue of multi-modal narratives and attempt to understand the qualitative differences, if any, in processing them.

> Hence the emergence of new questions for post-classical narratology: What sense-making possibilities do multimodal storytelling practices afford that are not afforded by monomodal or single-channel narrative practices, and vice versa? What are the differences among the processing strategies required for multimodal narratives that exploit different semiotic channels, e.g., words and images versus utterances and gestures? (Herman, 2010, p. 95)

To put it more simply, we are only now beginning to understand the ways in which storytelling practices are affected by the use of multiple modes and media. From a narrative point of view, it is important to understand the possibilities and constraints of the different modes and media in order to be able to deploy the most appropriate narrative resources in context and to decide by what means to best express one's intended meaning. Chapter 2 will explore the affordances of the visual and the verbal and will examine their interaction in particular narrative contexts.

The Relative Importance of the Spatial and Temporal in Narrative

Even so-called monomodal texts, such as a printed narrative, have multimodal potential. As van Leeuwen (2004) points out, meanings can be made visually in written text through choice of layout or choice and size of font, for example.

Texts can be laid out in (relatively self-contained) blocks rather than in linear sequence, thus bringing to the fore their spatial rather than their temporal potential. A look at the homepage of the University of Surrey or indeed at almost any website is sufficient to understand what is meant by blocks of text. While clearly there is still a linear dimension to text – information is given in sequence and is normally hierarchically ordered in terms of priority – the layout is such as to suggest a different set of relations to those configured by 'purely' linear texts. As we will see in Chapter 3, reading paths are likely to be affected by manner of layout with the possibility of a new mapping of textual relations whereby positioning on the screen (marginal vs. central; top vs. bottom) and degree of prominence (as determined by size and type of font, for example) become the guiding navigational principles displacing a more or less linear trajectory.

Moreover, the possibility of combining verbal and visual resources in the composition of a narrative text can complicate the ways in which we process information and construct meanings. Given the different ways in which we might presume to approach verbal and visual texts, 'taking in' a photograph, for example, at a glance, as opposed to 'reading through' a stretch of text, their combination and interaction can serve to disrupt linearity and to construct an alternative reading path (Kress, 2003). As I shall argue in Chapter 2 with respect to Sebald's *Austerlitz*, the incorporation of a visual narrative in the verbal unfolding of events creates a disruption of the temporal at the same time as it leads to a temporalization of the spatial insofar as some of the images can be seen to relate to one another both prospectively and retrospectively.

Emphasizing the spatial potentials of narrative text and the construction of a storyworld in terms of a kind of virtual or mental universe having both spatial extension and temporal duration is intended not to undermine notions of narrative time and time in narrative but simply to point to some of the ways in which narratives may be changing. Clearly events (either fictional or real) and their depiction take place in and over time and readers attend to chronology in their reconstruction of what happens when in a narrative representation. The manner in which events are sequenced and the choice of where to start a narrative – for example, at the beginning, at the end or in medias res – can affect a reader's perception of events, their interrelationship, their causes and consequences. For example, Sarah Waters's decision to reverse the chronology of *The Night Watch*, a story set in the 1940s, and move backwards through time (from 1947 to 1944 to 1941) has the effect of focusing the reader's attention on how current states of affairs came into being and creates a kind of inevitability with respect to the stasis and disillusionment felt by the characters in the present.

In addition, the process of reading takes place in and over time and readers must anticipate what comes next as well as hold in memory what they have already read. This dynamic between what has been (memory) and what is yet to come (anticipation) is part of what is involved in the act of reading and what we hold in memory comes to condition understanding of present contingencies as well as future possibilities. As Ricoeur puts it:

> Looking back from the conclusion to the episodes leading up to it, we have to be able to say that this ending required these sorts of events and this chain of actions. But this backward look is made possible by the teleological movement directed by our expectations when we follow a story. (Ricoeur, 2000, p. 259)

For Ricoeur (2000, p. 261), 'narrative activity is the privileged discursive expression of preoccupation and its making present' by which I understand him to be referring to the way in which the nowness of the present asserts itself not in relation to abstract concepts of time but in relation to a kind of motivated activity and concern with the circumstances and consequences of our being in time.

Perceptions of time and the ways in which situations and circumstances change with time can be represented in numerous ways within a narrative and indeed techniques for representing a character's changing interaction with the world around him/her and his/her experience of time are many and various. As Herman (2002, p. 215) points out, while 'rigidly bracketing the telling from the told [. . .] could [. . .] vitiate the phenomenology of reading', distinguishing story time and discourse time or the events of the story and the manner of their narration can be useful in pointing to the ways in which particular effects are achieved.

Questions of duration, frequency and order (Genette, 1983) are important in helping to pace the narrative and in setting out particular types of relations between story and discourse. If, for example, a scene is described in detail rather than briefly summarized, it may suggest that it is of significance in the greater scheme of things; or if a period of time in a character's life is elided, the reader may conclude that nothing of much relevance to the plot has happened in the intervening years. Likewise, the frequency with which an event is recounted may have a bearing on a reader's understanding of its impact on a character or characters within the narrative. And, as already mentioned, presentation of events in an ordered sequence or via analepses (flashbacks) or prolepses (flashforwards) can affect a reader's interpretation of the 'logic' of the story and its motivating force.

Given that much narrative terminology and its more technical aspects were derived predominantly from detailed analyses of works of literary fiction, the question of its continued relevance to evolving forms of narrative across modes and media is a legitimate one. I have already suggested the usefulness of insights stemming from domains such as multimodality in providing ways of framing questions and reflecting on issues pertinent to developments in contemporary narrative.

The Relationship between Narrative and Genre

Genre, like narrative, is a term with a long history and a diversity of use and application. This leads to different understandings and usages among specialists in different domains. For example, within the context of English literature, genre is often used to refer to 'the novel', 'drama' and 'poetry' as representative of the different branches of literature and literary production. Where the term genre fiction is used, it often refers to such things as 'the romance', 'the western' or 'the detective novel' and is usually contrasted, by virtue of a focus on entertainment, with the high artistic aspirations of literary fiction. However, such distinctions all too easily break down in the wake of literary history which points to the ways in which works originally tagged as genre fiction enter the literary canon and are seen as part and parcel of an evolving literary tradition (e.g. the works of Edgar Allan Poe in relation to detective fiction).

As Pyrhönen (2007, p. 109) points out, the term genre can be used to refer to 'principled groupings of text' or to a 'shared conception' of the features of particular types of text which feed and conform to a reader's expectations and guide interpretation of what s/he is reading, as well as providing a roadmap for writers wishing to contribute to a particular genre. Genre can be seen as either 'descriptive' or 'prescriptive', the former in relation to attempts to uncover the characteristics of particular types of text, the latter insofar as identification of the dominant features of a genre may be read as law and, therefore, suggest requirement rather than preference or be viewed as an evolving state of affairs permitting changes over time.

That ideas about genre do change over time is evidenced by the different notions of genre held in classical times compared to those prevalent among the Romantics, for example. As Pyrhönen (2007) points out, classical models saw genres as stable and universal entities, whereas for the Romantics genres were 'historically determined, dynamic entities' (p. 111) described in metaphors that emphasized their ability to grow, flower and even die. The Romantics began to rebel against what they saw as 'the supposed rigidity of traditional generic rules' viewing them as 'tyrannical constraints upon an author's individual feeling and sensibility' (p. 112).

The idea of genre as a resource for meaning-making rather than a restrictive set of conventions will be pursued here. Interest will lie in the ways in which writers draw on generic conventions, while manipulating them for their own purposes, and in the extent to which reader expectations are fulfilled or subverted. Insofar as narrative is seen to refer to the kind of text which charts changes in a state of affairs over time, changes which are seen to impact upon a sentient being or beings and to be attributable to a particular cause or causes, the novel would appear to be a narrative prototype. However, as we have seen, narrative, in the sense of a story presented by a narrator or narrators, is not exclusive to the printed word but can be realized on the screen (both big and small) and can be relayed orally in face-to-face settings or transmitted by audio or audio-visual means. The printed book, as medium, while it may contribute to the forms in which narrative is realized and may constrain or afford particular narrative possibilities, is not co-extensive with narrative. There-fore, if we consider the novel as a genre, it does not follow that narrative and genre are the same thing, since narrative extends to more than the novel form and can be realized across modes and media.

The Relationship between Narrative and Gender

Page (2007) summarizes the issues in respect of narrative and gender pointing to feminist criticism of a perceived male obsession with abstraction and, in some instances, highly technical categorization of narrative. In addition, she flags up the prototypical narrative trajectory whereby a subject (usually male) seeks and finds an object (usually female) as a result of a quest beset by obstacles and conflicts which the protagonist has to overcome in order to enjoy his prize. Clearly, while not all protagonists are male, the history of the novel can be seen to be dominated by male authors, if not male characters, for largely social and economic reasons. As Woolf (1981) reminds us, the lack of a room of one's own and an annual stipend is likely to make it more difficult for women to enjoy the same opportunities as men in respect of writing fiction.

In addition, given that the characteristic features of narrative have been derived from a largely male corpus, there is the view that it is unrepresentative and that writing by women may display different characteristics. For example, metaphors of flow and flux or of fragmentation and disruption are often associated with novels by women in contrast to the drive towards a clear conclusion evidenced in narratives by men. As Page (2007, p. 199) points out, however, such a view is still highly contested by critics and indeed by novelists themselves. As we will see in relation to Woolf's work as well as that by her literary heirs, such as Winterson and Ali Smith, issues of gender and sexuality are quite often thematized in their work and, as is often the case with Woolf's work, coherence lies at the level of metaphor and image rather than at the level of plot. This tendency to realize the potential of narrative at levels other than those of story and plot but at the level of language and image, thus creat-ing poetic and metaphorical links between what might otherwise be discrete sections of a novel is typical of modernist (and some postmodernist) interest in the connections and intersections between the visual and the verbal, the spatial and the temporal. This is a strand in narrative which continues to be explored by both male and female authors in the wake of recognition of language as just one of many modes which can be exploited to communicate and express meaning.

The Relationship between the History of Narrative and the History of the Novel

I have already referred to the tendency of classic narratology to focus analysis on literary works (e.g. Barthes's analysis of a short story, *Sarrasine*, by Balzac), even while recognizing the narrative qualities of other types of text (e.g. advertisements; magazines). This was partly the result of an attempt to identify the 'literary' and the 'non-literary' and to build typologies of different genres (e.g. detective fiction). In addition, because the early narratologists tended to come from literary studies or neighbouring disciplines (social anthropology, philosophy; linguistics), literature tended to be the primary object of their enquiry. However, post-classical approaches to narrative have come from a broad range of disciplines, as a result of which the field of study has widened considerably.

Furthermore, the production of narratives drawing on multiple modes and media alongside growing interest in adaptation (cf. Hutcheon, 2006) have led to a situation where the resources, features, purposes, transpositions and transformations of narrative are exciting renewed efforts to understand the dynamics of narrative and the mechanisms by which it has evolved. As Herman (2007, p. 16) points out, there is 'an emergent concern with how medium-specific properties of stories may require the adjustment and refinement of classical models'. Insofar as the present book aims to look at the forces shaping narrative production today and to link these forces to features of the narrative texts produced, it seeks to contribute to this endeavour.

In the chapters which follow, I shall examine more closely the various dimensions of narrative which I see as significant in its evolution. Chapter 2 will focus on the potentials of the visual and verbal modes and of their intersection in the construction of narrative. It will also explore further the issue of temporality and spatialization in relation to contemporary narrative tendencies. Chapter 3 will focus on the role of media, in addition to mode, in effecting narrative change and will look at the requirements of processes of adaptation.

Chapter 4 will address the material specificity of narrative in relation to the availability of resources such as language/s and culture/s and examine the consequences for narrative of multilingualism and multiculturalism. Chapter 5 will continue the theme of resources for narrative and will suggest that the default position for narrative is one of transposition and transformation in relation to existing narrative texts. From this perspective, genre will be seen to be fluid rather than fixed and a source of creativity rather than a set of restrictions or prohibitions. The final chapter will take this forward in relation to a discussion of some of the ways in which a narrative 'unmooring' in relation to its disciplinary and generic base can be liberating and productive.

Chapter 2

Intermodal Translation: Verbal and Visual Narratives

Setting the Scene

The introductory chapter has served to set the scene in terms of developments in narrative theory and practice and has identified areas where there continue to be arguments about the relative importance of some aspects of narrative, including, for example, with respect to understandings of temporality and spatiality. The present chapter will return to these areas in relation to the question of how images can be harnessed both singly and in series to construct a narrative. More specifically, it will explore current interest in the affordances and constraints of the visual and the verbal (Kress, 2003; Kress and van Leeuwen, 2006) and examine the ways in which writers avail themselves of visual and verbal resources in their work to tell particular types of stories and convey a point of view. The focus will be on how text and image interact and on the effects of such interaction in terms of the production and reception of meaning.

It is perhaps important to spell out what we mean by image and to look more closely at the particularities of the visual and verbal modes. Writers have long used verbal resources to describe the setting in which a particular story takes place and to create or re-create for the reader a sense of place. For example, the beginning of Dickens's *Great Expectations* sketches out the characteristics of the area in which Pip grows up and depicts the graveyard in which he has a rather frightening encounter with Magwitch, the escaped convict.

Ours was the marsh country, down by the river, within, as the river wound, twenty miles of the sea. My first most vivid and broad impression of the identity of things, seems to me to have been gained on a memorable raw afternoon towards evening. At such a time I found out for certain, that this bleak place overgrown with nettles was the churchyard; [. . .] and that the dark flat wilderness beyond the churchyard, intersected with dykes and mounds and gates, with scattered cattle feeding on it, was the marshes; and that the low leaden line beyond, was the river; and that the distant savage lair from which the wind was rushing, was the sea; and that the small bundle of shivers growing afraid of it all and beginning to cry, was Pip. (Dickens, 1986, p. 35)

There are a number of things to say about this short passage both in relation to its translation of the visual and its narrative function. First, it illustrates the way in which one prominent nineteenth-century novelist has chosen to create a sense of place through description. Through the use of adjectives and the positioning of one element of the landscape in relation to another, the reader gets a sense of type and extent of the terrain in which this first scene takes place and learns something of the effect of the landscape on the young Pip. Within the larger context of the novel, narrated by the older Pip, as he remembers his younger self, the opening pages serve to situate him socially as well as geographically – we learn that he has lost his parents and is being brought up by his sister and her husband – and to contextualize his narration of an experience which was to prove pivotal – his encounter with Magwitch who would turn out, years later, to be his benefactor. In addition, a note (note 1, p. 499) makes clear that the setting for Dickens's novel corresponds in some degree to the places known to the author and that he most likely 'combined memories of several small villages lying between Gad's Hill and the Thames' (p. 499). Without wishing to embark on a discussion of realism, which is not the subject of this book, I would simply point to the phenomenon whereby writers tend to draw on aspects of their own experience, including the physical environment, as a resource in the construction of their work.

This example serves not to raise the question of a correspondence between the 'real' and the verbally realized image depicted in the book but rather as an illustration of the ability of language to trigger or cue images in our minds. Here the images relate most obviously to a geographical setting in which actions take place but they also serve to convey a psycho-geography in the sense of a tendency to associate particular places with specific moods and feelings as well as with incidents and events. Pip clearly finds the landscape and the graveyard frightening. The place is 'bleak', the graveyard 'overgrown with nettles'; the late afternoon is 'raw' and the wind is howling. Altogether it is a most inhospitable and 'savage' place, likely to stir feelings of fear in a young boy. It is also the perfect backdrop against which to set Pip's encounter with Magwitch, that 'fearful man, all in coarse grey, with a great iron on his leg' (p. 36).

Words, then, clearly have the potential to evoke images of place, and indeed of character, whether those places or characters are real or imagined or a combination of both. Eco (2003) devotes a chapter in his book on Translation to a discussion of the ways in which writers attempt to create visual effects through language and points to its ancient pedigree. His discussion of hypotyposis and ekphrasis illustrates the problems associated with rendering in words what one sees (pp. 104–22). He examines the various techniques used by writers to create visual effects and evaluates their effectiveness in relation to original works and their translation. In the context of a work on translation as negotiation, Eco is primarily concerned with how one might render in language B effects achieved in language A; however, he is also concerned with the ways in which writers move from the visual to the verbal and with the functioning of verbally

realized images in text. It is in the latter sense that his work is most clearly
relevant to the present discussion.

Drawing on one mode to convey or prompt a sense of the other is not just the
prerogative of writers. Film-makers also need to think about how to translate
words into images, what to show and what to tell, in their work. This is particularly true in respect of adaptations, as we will see in greater detail in Chapter 3,
but even if s/he works from an original screenplay, the director will be conscious of making shooting and editing decisions in relation to the affordances
and constraints of the particular mode and medium. Whereas images of places
and characters are determinate and concrete in film, they must be evoked or
triggered through language in a verbal text. Therefore an ability to understand
the potentials and limitations of the verbal and the visual will be important
in constructing aspects of an unfolding tale, whether that tale be delivered by
verbal or by visual means or indeed by a combination of the two.

Returning to our example of *Great Expectations*, it is clear that a film version of
the novel will show, rather than describe, the landscape and scenery. In David
Lean's (1946) classic version of *Great Expectations*, for example, the viewer sees a
long shot of the marshes and a boy running. He runs past the gallows, register-
ing them as he goes, and clambers over a wall into the graveyard to tend his
parents' grave. The wind is howling and the trees are creaking. A tree, at which
the boy looks up, appears to loom over him; the trunk is so gnarled that
it appears to have a face on it. The boy starts to run away and bumps into
Magwitch, who seizes him and towers over him. It is at this point that the
dialogue begins.

That the film is based on a book is made clear right from the beginning of the
film which features a shot of the first page of a book, the first line of which is
read out as a voice-over; subsequent pages are then quickly flicked through to
signal the end of the novel and the beginning of the story as it will be realized
cinematographically. The play of light and dark – Lean's film was shot in black and
white – serves to foreground some compositional elements, such as the gallows
and the looming tree, which are clearly outlined and brought to our attention.
The shadowy atmosphere and sense of bleakness and ominousness are created
through choice, length and angle of shot (e.g. the gallows, the looming tree) as
well as through facial expression (e.g. the young boy's nervous gaze).

The theory and practice of intermodal or intersemiotic translation is clearly
of relevance in moving from one sign system to another and for understanding
the functional specialization of one mode as opposed to another in multimodal
texts (Kress, 2003). In other words, knowing what information or idea is carried
visually and what is carried verbally as well as what is likely to happen in the
process of their interaction is important for both the production and reception
of text. The incorporation of both visual and verbal resources into a narrative
text has the potential to extend the narrative repertoire and to provide greater
differentiation and/or greater depth of experience depending on how well
realized the text is as a whole.

Clearly, the cultural and social context is an important component in the 'mix'. It is often said that we in the West live in a society where the image is ubiquitous and dominant and where information and ideas are increasingly conveyed in visual form (Kress, 2003). Concomitantly, the kinds of literacy practices on which we have depended are changing with a move away from the dominance of writing towards an ability to function multimodally in the new media age (Kress, 2003). That forms of communication in general are changing in the twenty-first century is perhaps uncontentious insofar as we see the evidence before us: blogs and wikis are now an established part of newsroom routines and political life; there is greater interactivity between audiences and programme makers and between audiences and programme participants; and the computer is now at the heart of most businesses, educational establishments and financial services. Indeed it is difficult to imagine life without communication technologies.

What is perhaps less obvious is the extent to which narrative practices may also be changing as a result of the possibilities afforded by the new technologies which allow writers to incorporate into their texts visual images, diagrams, drawings and other realia, thereby transforming them, even at a superficial level. To take just one recent example: in Xiaolu Guo's (2009) *UFO in Her Eyes*, the story, which takes place in rural China and revolves around the apparent sighting by a peasant woman of a UFO, is related in the form of case notes and interviews with the reproduction of files, transcripts, documents and diagrams. Visually, the work is arresting since it does not conform to expectations of what a work of fiction might look like in terms of 200–300 pages of continuous prose divided into sequential chapters. Rather it subverts generic expectations right from the start by presenting what look like dossiers held by the National Security and Intelligence Agency containing transcripts of interviews relating to a particular event and its aftermath.

Yet the unorthodox framing and presentation of the narrative does not ultimately undermine its narrative structure. What we have in a somewhat different-than-expected form is the story of what happens to the inhabitants of a small village in China as a consequence of an event – the alleged sighting of a UFO – which initiates all sorts of changes in the lives of the villagers. The main tenets of an unfolding narrative are still present. We have a change in a state of affairs, a before and an after, we have characters whose lives are disrupted by an event and its aftermath and we have an indication of a point of view. What the presentation of the situation in the form of dossiers allows is both an interrogation of a dramatic situation and its containment within a particular locale. At the same time, the work trades on the creation of a certain verisimilitude by drawing on our world knowledge of China as a country on the verge of great technological and economic development yet with a hinterland of agrarianism and pre-industrial ignorance and superstition. The secrecy which might be expected to surround such a sighting and the subsequent containment of the village provide a somewhat humorous context for examination of the cost of globalization to China and allows for the unfolding of a human drama.

In other words, while the form of Guo's narrative appears initially not to conform to that of a conventional tale, its substance and dynamic ultimately follow a recognizable pattern in spite of certain textual and generic innovations. The inclusion of visual and graphic material in this instance appears to be motivated by an attempt to mimic a plausible response to an unusual and highly irregular situation and to help embed the apparent sighting of a UFO in a work concerned not with science fiction and dystopian futures but with current processes of globalization and their effects on traditional ways of life in rural China.

Sebald's *Austerlitz*

A more complex case of inclusion of the visual and, more specifically, the interaction of visual and verbal modes in the construction of a narrative can be found in the work of W. G. Sebald. The book on which I shall focus in this instance is Sebald's (2002a) *Austerlitz*, described as a 'literary tour de force' (Saumarez Smith, 2001). There are a number of issues worthy of discussion in connection with *Austerlitz* in addition to the question of the visual–verbal interaction, issues which have an important bearing on contemporary understandings of narrative. Like some of Sebald's other works, *The Rings of Saturn* (2002b), for example, *Austerlitz* is a work which seems to defy easy categorization. Part historical odyssey, part fictional memoir, it relates the story of one man's discovery of his true identity and his eventual confrontation with the uncomfortable and traumatic 'facts' of his existence.

Rather than being told directly, the story of Austerlitz is related in instalments by a narrator who acts as a kind of mediator between reader and protagonist in that he relays conversations held with Austerlitz over a number of years. To begin with, the substance of these conversations relating as they do to architectural history appear to have little to do with the more personal history of Austerlitz which is eventually uncovered. However, it becomes clear that the professional and intellectual concerns of Austerlitz – his interest in military fortifications, prisons and railway stations and his obsession with categorization and the creation of networks of knowledge – do have a bearing on his family history, biography and sense of self. For he comes to understand that his exclusive focus on architecture up to and including the nineteenth century has, in some ways, been a means of systematically avoiding references to and discussion of more recent twentieth-century European history which, as he discovers, was to have such a devastating personal effect. It is in an antiquarian bookstore near the British Museum that he is forced to recognize that the memories being evoked by two voices on the radio with respect to the special transport of children in the summer of 1939 from the Hook of Holland to Harwich are memories which he shares:

> only then did I know beyond any doubt that these fragments of memory were part of my own life as well. (Sebald, 2002a, p. 200)

This is the moment when he decides to go in search of his own history and sets out for Prague where he finds his old nurse Vera and begins to piece his story together from what she tells him.

In terms of narrative structure, the insistence throughout *Austerlitz* on relaying information at second hand, so to speak, in that conversations are recalled and mediated, does not appear arbitrary but rather seems to be a deliberate strategy for keeping things at a distance. The reader is constantly reminded that what is being transmitted is a report, albeit a very detailed one, of what was said, seen and done. The narrative spins a kind of web which evokes aspects of the past and transmits them like pieces of a jigsaw puzzle to be slotted into shape. Similar to the use of Brechtian *Verfremdungseffekt* (alienation technique or distancing effect) the reader is kept at arm's length by the reporting structure, a series of Chinese boxes whereby even conversations-within-conversations are conveyed (e.g. 'And I remember, Vera told me, said Austerlitz' (Sebald, 2002a, p. 226)).

The almost manic inclusion of a reporting tag – Austerlitz began; said Austerlitz; Austerlitz continued – serves to disrupt a tendency to imagine a storyworld and immerse oneself in it and reminds the reader of the verbal nature of what is being related. This is a story told by a homodiegetic narrator, that is, by one who is also a protagonist in a drama – though a somewhat incidental one, since his role is largely that of listener and reporter/scribe – about someone else. That someone else – Austerlitz – is the focus of our interest, as his personal history is unravelled against the backdrop of a (for him) forgotten or submerged European history.

In narrative terms, Austerlitz is the object of focalization and while at times we have the illusion that he is recounting his own story, we are constantly reminded by the interventions of the narrator that this story is being recounted by another after the fact. That there be a temporal gap between thoughts and actions and their articulation and elaboration is not unusual in narrative; what is striking in this instance is the insistence on temporal displacement through use of the reporting tag and the creation of a spatial dimension to the narrative by means of a kind of mise en abyme whereby one piece of discourse is framed by and contained within another. From a deconstructive perspective, we might interpret this as the inability of discourse to refer to anything other than itself and an undermining of the project of academics like Austerlitz to name and categorize the world with a view to ordering and controlling it. Austerlitz's carefully controlled universe comes apart when the real intrudes

on the symbolic order he has created. The fragments of memory stowed away
come back to haunt him and he sees again his five-year-old self 'waiting on a
quay in a long crocodile of children lined up two by two, most of them carrying
rucksacks or small leather cases' (Sebald, 2002a, p. 200).

The significance of the rucksack as both container of Austerlitz's few posses-
sions and as a kind of identity marker is made clear in the course of the narrative. The narrator's first sighting of Austerlitz after a gap of almost 20 years
at Liverpool Street Station sees him unchanged in carriage and clothing with
'the rucksack still slung over his shoulder' (p. 54). It is the presence of the
rucksack, so the narrator believes, along with 'the horror-stricken expressions
on both their faces' (p. 55) that cause him to see in Austerlitz a resemblance
to the philosopher, Ludwig Wittgenstein. We learn that Wittgenstein, like
Austerlitz, always carried a rucksack, an object which came to be identified with
him so closely that in a letter to him his sister told him that it was almost as
dear to her as his person. The narrator comes to equate Wittgenstein and
Austerlitz and to see in the image of one the person of the other.

Relatively early on in the narrative, the reader learns that Austerlitz's rucksack was bought at an army surplus store on the Charing Cross Road for ten
shillings just before he began his studies and that he considers it 'the only
truly reliable thing in his life' (p. 55). A photograph of a rucksack, reproduced
on the page where the narrator tells us of the provenance of Austerlitz's rucksack and indicates his physical resemblance to Wittgenstein, might appear to
have a purely illustrative function when in fact we later recognize its totemic
power. For on arrival in Britain, Austerlitz carried a little rucksack which then
disappeared after he went to live with his foster parents in Bala, Wales. Its 'disappearance' or removal comes to symbolize loss of something valuable and to
stand for an absence at the core of his existence.

In an antiquarian bookstore, as he listens to the voices coming from the
radio which 'cast such a spell' (p. 199), he begins to visualize aspects of his past
life and to unearth images of that fateful day in which he left his mother in
Prague and set out via the Hook of Holland for a new life in Britain.

> I saw the great slabs of paving at my feet again, the mica in the stone, the
> grey-brown water in the harbour basin, the ropes and anchor chains slanting
> upwards, the bows of the ship, higher than a house, the seagulls fluttering
> over our heads and screeching wildly, the sun breaking through the clouds,
> and the red-haired girl in the tartan cape and velvet beret who had looked
> after the smaller children in our compartment during the train journey
> through the dark countryside. (pp. 200–1)

These images, related verbally, are evocative of the perspective of a small boy
as he recalls a departure by ship, one which was to prove definitive, after a long
train journey in the darkness.

In Prague, as he makes his way to the house where he had spent his early days, memories begin to come back to him in a Proustian way through the senses (pp. 212–13) and he finds himself in 'a state of blissful yet anxious confusion' (p. 215), as he deciphers 'signs and characters from the type-case of forgotten things' (p. 214), the cool air in the hallway, the metal box for the electrics, the rise of the stairs and so on. Through Vera's accounts, he is able to fill in details of his past and to recover some early memories. Vera also discovers a couple of photos which she gives to Austerlitz: one showing the stage of a provincial theatre – his mother had been an opera singer – the other showing Austerlitz himself dressed as if for a fancy ball. Despite scrutinizing the photo in great detail and at length, Austerlitz finds it difficult to identify with his younger self. Rather he feels as if the younger boy is demanding of him that he avert the tragedy about to happen (p. 260).

Kress and van Leeuwen's (2006) terminology in respect of how we read images and the grammar of visual design is useful in helping to analyse Austerlitz's reaction to what he sees. The photograph clearly has a narrative, as opposed to conceptual, representational structure (p. 59). It features an actor, a young boy, dressed in a white pageboy costume, who occupies the centre of the photograph, thus signalling that he is the focus of interest. His gaze is looking outward, demanding to be met (cf. demand vs. offer).

In looking at the photograph so many years later, Austerlitz reacts to the directionality of the gaze of the young pageboy and feels powerless to avert the tragedy yet to come in relation to the moment at which the photo was taken, that is six months before Austerlitz was sent to England on the Kindertransport (children's transport). The low-angle of the camera makes the figure of the pageboy more prominent and potentially more powerful or mesmerizing from the viewer's perspective. The setting, which Austerlitz struggles to make out, appears generic – grass in the foreground; the background fuzzy and out of focus. He thinks it is some kind of field but has no idea where it is/was. From the writing on the back and from Vera's explanatory words, he understands that he was a pageboy carrying the train of his mother dressed as the Rose Queen at a masked ball at the house of one of her admirers but he cannot place the event or recall himself in the role.

> Yet hard as I tried both that evening and later, I could not recollect myself in the part. I did recognize the unusual hairline running at a slant over the forehead, but otherwise all memory was extinguished in me by an over-whelming sense of the long years that had passed. (Sebald, 2002a, p. 259)

This quotation is of interest for a number of reasons. First, it calls attention to recognition on Austerlitz's part that the image shares something 'objective' with himself – the unusual hairline. Yet, even so, the distance between his younger self and the person he has become is so vast that he cannot seem to bridge the temporal gap. As Sontag (1977, p. 16) puts it in relation to the nature and role of the photograph:

> A photograph is both a pseudo-presence and a token of absence. Like a wood fire in a room, photographs – especially those of people, of distant landscapes and faraway cities, of the vanished past – are incitements to reverie.

Austerlitz sees that his younger self was present at an event of which he has no conscious memory. In this sense, he is both 'there' and 'not there', since the context is missing. Sontag goes on to talk about the photograph's 'attempt to contact or lay claim to another reality' (p. 16). In essence, this is what Austerlitz is trying to do: to make contact with his forgotten past; however, despite the materiality and presence of the photograph, the past which it recalls remains unavailable to him. He cannot put himself back into the role he was playing at the time. The slice of life or the moment which the photograph aimed to capture does not give up its story. The story has to be told.

For Kress (2003), one of the differences between the visual and verbal modes is the fact that the visual presents to us a given, something determinate, unlike language which he sees as more schematic, demanding to be filled in. We 'take in' at a glance the dimensions and colouring of a painting, while language has to be 'coloured in' and images realized as we read from left to right and top to bottom, at least in respect of Western languages. What Kress is pointing to can best be understood in relation to the phenomenon of adaptation where sometimes the film of a book can be disappointing partly because it makes concrete what is otherwise left to our imagination. Yet for Austerlitz the 'pres-entness' of the image of his younger self remains shrouded in mystery and has to be coloured in by the stories surrounding it.

There is, then, a kind of paradox in relation to the 'evidence' furnished by photographs. As a record of what has been, they appear to testify to the 'truth' of a past moment. At the same time, photographs, as Sontag (1977, p. 80) reminds us, are contingent and arbitrary. They are artefacts and relics with 'the status of found objects' (p. 69) which 'trade simultaneously on the prestige of art and the magic of the real' (p. 69). By 'prestige of art', I take Sontag to mean that the photograph selects material and the photographer composes a scene, more or less artfully depending on skill, expertise and pur-pose. In terms of 'the magic of the real', we can think of what Vera says as she hands the photographs to Austerlitz. She speaks about their 'mysterious quality [. . .] when they surface from oblivion' (Sebald, 2002a, p. 258) and of how they seem to have 'a memory of their own' (p. 258).

It is the photographs which appear to remember us and the roles that we played rather than the other way round. In other words, the relationship between past and present as triggered by and mediated in photographs appears to be complex. For Sontag (1977), a photograph 'is only a fragment, and with the passage of time its moorings come unstuck. It drifts away into a soft abstract pastness, open to any kind of reading' (p. 71). This may help to explain Austerlitz's difficulty in making sense of the photograph as an index of his own past. Too much time has elapsed for him to be able to 'fix' the photograph to the chain of his biography and so he looks at it as if the information it contains were historic, slightly alien and bearing little relation to self. The 'I' which he knows himself to have been becomes another, another who demands something of him which he is unable to give and so panic sets in (pp. 259–60).

The young pageboy in the photograph is, in this sense, a spectre, 'both spectacle and phantom' (Bal, 1997, p. 169). His fancy dress guarantees a kind of carnivalesque quality, while the contrast between light and dark, foreground and background serves to impress a certain unreality and ephemerality on the scene. Above the horizon is a 'blurred dark area' while 'the boy's curly hair [is] spectrally light around the outline of his head' (p. 259).

> As far back as I can remember, said Austerlitz, I have always felt as if I had no place in reality, as if I were not there at all, and I never had this impression more strongly than on that evening in the Šporkova when the eyes of the Rose Queen's page boy looked through me. (Sebald, 2002a, p. 261)

In terms of narrative, then, the inclusion of images in *Austerlitz* is complex and multifaceted. Some images, like that of the pageboy, clearly relate to the unfolding storyline which treats the main protagonist's breakdown and decision to explore his origins and the traumatic past from which he emerged. At one level, the recovery of the image provides evidence of a past existence and is testimony to another time, place and identity. Yet Austerlitz's inability to identify with the young boy in the photograph across the temporal and historic abyss that separates them points to the insufficiency of photographs to reveal their story and of the need for the 'evidence' which they contain to be supplemented and narrativized. The photograph is not autonomous in this sense in spite of its independent material existence but depends on the consciousness of a human subject being directed at it and engaging with it. The story it tells has to be recovered and contextualized, a process which requires the construction of a narrative thread. The visual thus depends upon the verbal and stands in an intimate relation with it.

Other images like that of the rucksack yield their meaning only retrospectively and in view of a layering of experience. It is an object's connotative, rather than denotative, value which is important or what Barthes calls the rhetoric of the image (Barthes, 1977, pp. 46–51). Rather than being present in photographs, meanings are made relative to the context in which they appear and the manner in which they are presented. Barthes recognizes, however, the distinctive contribution made by the photograph to the kind of consciousness developed by and in humans.

> The type of consciousness the photograph involves is indeed truly unprecedented, since it establishes not a consciousness of the *being-there* of the thing (which any copy could provoke) but an awareness of its *having-been-there*. What we have is a new space-time category: spatial immediacy and temporal anteriority, the photograph being an illogical conjunction between the *here-now* and the *there-then*. (Barthes, 1977, p. 44; italics in original)

In reading an unfolding narrative, we necessarily read from page to page and from moment to moment. This more or less sequential experience is interrupted by the inclusion of images whether they be photographs, stills, diagrams or other memorabilia or realia. The space occupied by the image and the way in which its substance must be 'read' require a pause, if only momentary, in the verbal narrative. Narrative time is disrupted and the linear flow replaced by a 'taking in' of the object/s presented in space. Yet these images assume meaning/s not in isolation but relative to the surrounding text in which they are embedded and relative to their place in the storyline of which they form a part.

In addition, some images speak to one another, such as the photo of Austerlitz's room (Sebald, 2002a, p. 43) and the photo of the record room in the fortress of Terezín where the files on the prisoners were kept (pp. 396–7). In contrast to Austerlitz's office, which is messy, with books spilling out of shelves, and almost every available surface covered in books or files or both, leaving little space for either himself or his students, the record office of Terezín is extremely tidy and orderly with files, systematically classified, occupying pigeon holes of equal size which line the walls from top to bottom. The surfaces are empty of clutter and the chairs grouped round tables are ready to be occupied if need be. The overall impression, however, is one of sterility and of orderliness devoid of humanity, an impression reinforced by our knowledge of the purpose of the camp to which the detainees were sent. By contrast Austerlitz's room, while also unoccupied, signals a very real human, if slightly chaotic, presence.

The images, while coming from different parts of the book and carrying no explicit verbal link, nevertheless connect across time and space and provide a commentary on one another through contrast. In this sense, as I have argued elsewhere (Doloughan, 2005), there is a kind of temporalization of the spatial – it is over time and in relation to one another that configurations of associated meanings cluster around certain images. In addition, there is what might be called a spatialization of the temporal through the intercalation of visual images which serve to disrupt the reading of a linear narrative. For the visuals do not always occupy a separate or adjoining page but sometimes intrude in the midst of a sentence forcing their way into consciousness even before a sentence has been completed. Moreover, as previously mentioned, the frame narrative as well as the insistent reporting structure set up a narrative structure whereby one tale consists of and leads to another at a different narrative level and there are stories within stories.

As a result of the framing and narrative embedding, there is the possibility of a chain of evaluation. The narrator is sympathetic to Austerlitz – they share similar intellectual interests and over time become friends rather than acquaintances. As Austerlitz prepares to leave for Paris in search of his father, he gives the key to the Alderney Street property, where he lives, to the narrator. The narrator's interest in Austerlitz is evidenced by his precision and desire to report fully and accurately the substance of Austerlitz's disquisitions and personal history. The reader learns little about the narrator per se; his actions appear at times to be motivated by his fascination with Austerlitz and the places he has inhabited rather than by interests of his own.

Yet at the end of the book we find the narrator making another trip to Breendonk, the fortification which he had first visited in the summer of 1967 on meeting Austerlitz in Antwerp. Its significance in the light of Austerlitz's story becomes apparent retrospectively as does the narrator's reaction to his first visit when his legs begin to feel heavier as he advances down the long, dark corridors and becomes nauseous in the confines of one of the casemates. That this was a place of torture and interrogation is made clear by subsequent discussion; disclosure of the narrator's origins – he is originally from Southern Germany – becomes poignant, rather than incidental. On the second trip, the narrator takes out of his pocket and begins to read a book, given to him by Austerlitz, which tells the story of a colleague's search for his grandfather, a Jewish rabbi, whose family moved, after the rabbi's premature death, from Lithuania to South Africa. When the colleague returns to Lithuania to track down his family's roots, he finds very few traces of the family left but uncovers the history of the death camps. The narrator's role as listener and recorder of Austerlitz's history comes to take on added significance in the light of his positioning as a child who grew up in Germany after the war before moving away at the age of 20. In some ways both the narrator and Austerlitz are outsiders; it is perhaps understandable that they should form a bond. What makes their friendship more poignant, however, is the fact that they experienced the aftermath of a traumatic part of European history from very different positions.

Austerlitz's quest to find evidence of his origins and to track down information regarding his parents' fate in WWII leads him to sift through all kinds of archival material, documents and files. He even manages to get a copy of a film made about Theresienstadt, a ghetto in Bohemia, during its transformation by the SS in advance of a Red Cross visit in an attempt to 'dissimulate the true nature of their deportation policy' (p. 339). He pores over the film, even playing it in slow motion in order not to miss anything. Although his gaze fixes on a young woman whom he imagines to be 'the singer Agáta from my faint memories' (p. 351) and whose face 'seems to me both strange and familiar'

(p. 351), Vera's reaction on seeing a copy is to shake her head. However, he does manage to find a photograph of an anonymous actress in the Prague theatrical archives for 1938–39 which Vera recognizes 'without a shadow of a doubt' (p. 353). He gives a copy of the photo to the narrator as a memento before going to Paris to try and trace his father.

The role of the photograph as memento mori is pertinent here. As Sontag (1977, p. 70) writes:

> Photography is the inventory of mortality [. . .]. Photographs state the innocence, the vulnerability of lives heading toward their own destruction, and this link between photography and death haunts all photographs of people.

The aging process so evident in photographs of people from different periods in their lives reminds us of our own mortality. In the case of the photograph of the anonymous actress, there is an added poignancy given the fact that she appears not to have survived the war. In this respect her youth and beauty stand in stark contrast to the fate we can only imagine her to have suffered in a death camp. The spatial immediacy and temporal anteriority of which Barthes spoke is particularly poignant and imbues the photograph with a sense of tragedy. For the young woman in the photograph who invites our gaze is no longer among the living. The photograph is testament to her having existed but she has not had the luxury of being able to look back from the vantage point of old age on her younger self.

To Austerlitz, the photograph 'seemed to resemble my dim memory of my mother' (p. 353), the degree of qualification serving to underscore the sense of temporal distance and absence. The fact that no name has been attributed to the actress whose photo was found 'among letters, files on employees, programmes and faded newspaper cuttings' (p. 353), viewed in the light of our knowledge of the dehumanization practised by the Nazis in respect of the Jews, serves to highlight bureaucratic mechanisms of depersonalization. From this perspective, the photographic record is an important supplement, if not antidote, to the inadequacies and betrayals of language.

It is no accident that the prelude to Austerlitz's first breakdown is an inability to manipulate language. For a man whose career has been premised on reading and writing and who has always enjoyed organizing his thoughts on paper, such an experience must have been frightening. '[. . .] as soon as I so much as picked up a pencil the endless possibilities of language, to which I could once safely abandon myself, became a conglomeration of the most inane phrases' (Sebald, 2002a, p. 173). Reading, as well as writing, is affected and he struggles to comprehend what he reads. 'I could see no connections any more, the sentences resolved themselves into a series of separate words, the words into random sets of letters, the letters into disjointed signs' (Sebald, 2002a, pp. 175–6). Eventually he gives up and burns his papers and books, 'anything with my writing on it' (p. 176) and enjoys temporary relief. However, insomnia sets in and he embarks on his nocturnal walks through London, a state of affairs that continues for about a year. During this time he begins to see 'images from a faded world' (p. 180) and to imagine that he hears 'people behind my back speaking in a foreign tongue, Lithuanian, Hungarian, or something else with a very alien note to it' (p. 180). This period is characterized by 'a kind of heartache [. . .] caused by the vortex of past time' (p. 182).

Interestingly, it is at this time that he starts taking photographs of the dead who were excavated from underneath a taxi rank during demolition work at Broad Street Station and comes to feel 'as if the dead were returning from their exile and filling the twilight around me with their strangely slow but incessant to-ing and fro-ing' (p. 188). It is as if the past, which he has so successfully excluded through his 'defensive reactions' (p. 198), has come back to haunt him. The 'self-censorship of the mind' (p. 198) in which he has engaged for decades demanding as it did ever greater efforts leads to his breakdown in the summer of 1992.

His trip to Bohemia and initial attempts to uncover his own history at first promise answers to 'the sources of his distress' (p. 322), yet his states of anxiety recur some weeks after his return and he is powerless to do anything to militate against them. He begins to suffer severe panic attacks and one day collapses in Alderney Street, striking his head on the pavement. He is taken to St. Clement's and wakes up to find himself on one of the men's wards 'after [. . .] nearly three weeks of mental absence' (p. 323). Advised by a doctor before his eventual discharge from hospital to do some light physical, rather than academic, work, he takes up a job as assistant gardener in a council-run nursery and begins to recover.

It is during this time that he begins reading again and works his way through an 800-page volume by Adler on the setting up and organization of the Theresienstadt ghetto. Although the ghetto is described in great detail 'in its objective actuality', Austerlitz finds 'something incomprehensible and unreal about it' (p. 331); such is the enormity of the gap between the destructive ends and the organizational means of the ghetto. The thoroughness and systematicity with which the ghetto was organized in terms of working routines and the transport and provision of goods and services is difficult to grasp in relation to the ultimately destructive ends achieved by all this organizational mania. Extreme rationality appears to lead inevitably to destruction.

What Austerlitz has sensed and begins to understand is the extent to which high levels of abstraction and a zeal for categorization and organization have led not to human progress and enlightenment but to human destruction. The plan of Theresienstadt (pp. 328–9), a conceptual, rather than narrative, representation, to use Kress and van Leeuwen's (2006) terms, betrays little of the reality of existence for its Jewish inhabitants in its outline and topography. Yet Austerlitz's psycho-geographical encounters with places and their forgotten histories have given the lie to these abstract diagrammatic representations.

For all Austerlitz's attempts to keep the reality of his own situation at bay, the spirits of the past come back to haunt him. He can neither escape history nor his own biography. It is as if temporality has a spatial dimension. The past has extension not just within the spaces of memory and imagination but subsists in stratified layers in the topography of the real.

As we will see, this concern with a layering of the past and of what is hidden just below the surface as well as what is revealed by geography and by landscape is also the focus of Paul Seawright's work. As a photographer, he is clearly primarily interested in the visual, rather than the verbal, mode. However, there is overlap with some of Sebald's preoccupations insofar as Seawright's focus is on what representations of place reveal, and on what stories they tell and/or fail initially to disclose.

Seawright's *Hidden*

Hidden is a record of a photographic exhibition shown at the Imperial War Museum between 5 February and 30 March 2003. The exhibition comprised photographs of Afghanistan taken by Seawright in the summer of 2002 in response to a commission by the museum to 'respond to the terrorist attack of 11 September and the war in Afghanistan' (Vaizey, 2002). Working under the auspices of a number of organizations including Landmine Action and the UN, Seawright was able to access some of the more remote and dangerous regions of Afghanistan. The result is a series of photographs of landscapes, mostly devoid of people but featuring remnants of the apparatus of war such as spent cartridges and landmines. The photos, the majority of which are mono-chromatic and spartan, have an austere beauty in spite of the desolation and destruction of which they speak. 'I have always been fascinated by the invis-ible, the unseen, the subject that doesn't easily present itself to the camera' (Seawright, 2000, p. 63, quoted in Durden, 2003).

This quotation from Seawright is of interest in a number of respects. First, the assumption that the camera doesn't lie or that what we see is captured directly and without artifice by the camera is brought into question by the photographer himself. Seawright's remarks may suggest that the visible world is composed of surfaces or folds, some of which keep hidden from the viewer aspects of its reality or alternatively that reality itself is layered and multifaceted. In any case it points to the role of the photographer in trying to capture a hidden dimension of the visible world. This of course begs the question of how this process of disclosure might take place in the course of an encounter between a photographer and his subject and, by extension, between photo-graph and viewer.

A second source of interest lies in the fact that Seawright's quotation under-mines what Kress and van Leeuwen (2006, p. 163) describe as 'the belief in the objectivity of photographic vision' and 'the primacy which is accorded to visual perception generally in our culture' (p. 163) by demanding on the part of the viewer a sensitivity to the unseen. From this perspective, the visible world is supplemented by its other, which is invisible or at least 'doesn't easily present itself to the camera', to use Seawright's words. This suggests then that the role of the photographer is in fact to capture not just what is visible but what remains hidden and to yield to the viewer an aspect of a scene or landscape not ordinarily present. Just as language has a denotative and a connotative dimension, so too does the image insofar as what presents itself to the eye must be read against the grain of cultural and contextual factors. It also lends to the image a sense of depth: what appears on the surface is not necessarily the real subject of the photograph.

The process of reading Seawright's photographs requires not just an understanding of the affordances of the visual mode but also demands an appreciation of culture and context. As Durden (2003) puts it:

> In war-torn Afghanistan, Seawright is more concerned with the hidden malevolence of landscapes which have been heavily mined than the visible scars of war. The sense of pictorial innocence is brought out through his vistas of the desert, landscapes in which the very emptiness and uneventfulness radically undermines expectations of what a war zone looks like and most clearly counters the familiar media iconography of Afghanistan as a landscape of ruins.

As Durden suggests, Seawright's photographs need to be read against the grain of images, past and present, produced by Western photojournalists as well as in relation to the history of Afghanistan insofar as it is told by and filtered through the press. In this sense, the visual, as much as the verbal, is mediated by narrative conventions and shaped by cultural and contextual forces. The perspective on Afghanistan offered to the viewer by Seawright relates to what Durden calls a 'Poetics of Absence', by which he means to point to Seawright's tendency to index presence through absence and to trigger a sense of poignancy through visual modality and particular coding orientations (see Kress and van Leeuwen, 2006, pp. 160–3; pp. 165–6).

For example, in 'Camp Boundary' a huddle of tents has been pushed to the right-hand edge of the photograph such that it appears to be marginalized. There is no direct evidence of human habitation, though the very presence of tents indicates that people are likely to be sheltering there – Durden indicates that it is a refugee camp. In the foreground can be seen harsh, stony terrain; the background shows a high mountain sweeping down to some barely visible foothills. Because of the sheer scale and extent of the mountains in comparison with the size of the tents which they dwarf, a sense of the vulnerability of humans in such a landscape is suggested. The soft-focus of the background compared to the clarity with which the stony foreground is presented suggests a certain unreality in addition to vast distance. Granted it may well be early morning before people have risen with the mountains still hazy in the distance; however, the monochromatic effect with little colour differentiation and a predominance of browns, greys and bleached-out sky give the photograph an almost ghostly or ethereal quality.

Another series of photographs shows empty rooms, the majority shot from inside dilapidated buildings looking out at the bleached-out sky. Durden (2003) indicates that these bombed-out structures were former Taliban barracks and suggests that 'the uncanny repetition of the damage, much as it might make us think about the clinical precision of US bombing, also becomes significant and meaningful in relation to Afghanistan's history of repeated destruction and suffering'. The one exception to the series is 'Room VII' which shows a door opening onto a room with a table and two chairs positioned diagonally opposite one another. While there is no indication of what the room was used for, the photographic layout – the viewer sees the room from a slightly oblique angle through an aperture provided by the door which is slightly ajar – and choice of dark colours and play of light and shadow suggest that the room was used for sinister purposes, possibly an interrogation. It is the absence of human subjects that helps create a sense of menace and malevolence.

Absence and emptiness recur as leitmotifs throughout the series of photographs. In 'Desert Road' a raised track cuts through the desert. The paved portion in the foreground on the left-hand side comes to a sudden end but the track continues tapering off into the distance. The surface is uneven and the ground cracked and stony suggesting a bumpy ride. To either side of the road lies the vast expanse of desert. A few hardy looking plants appear to line the sides of the road in the foreground but otherwise the land looks harsh and arid. The bleached-out sky with tinges of a bluer hue on the edges occupies two-thirds of the picture. The absence of strong colour saturation and the minimal colour differentiation serve to imbue the photo with a sense of timelessness and stillness at odds with what we know of the hidden dangers of the landscape just beneath the surface and evidence of which we find in other photographs in the series such as 'Mounds' and 'Valley'.

Seawright's photographs, then, present to the viewer an account of aspects of the conflict in Afghanistan from the perspective of a Westerner who is an observer of, rather than a participant in, the war. However, his photographs attempt to tell a story of the country's history of suffering and point to the continuance of hidden dangers (e.g. from minefields) just below the surface. As Durden (2003) puts it:

> Seawright replays a pictorialism associated and embedded in past traditions of representing the desert landscape, and reveals it for what it is at the same time, a protective screen, a poetic filter, from a violent reality which cannot find adequate representation. The violence in these landscapes of mine-fields is still to come, present but hidden, primed, a future devastation.

Seawright arrives after many of the conflicts and battles are over, but still represents something 'live'.

As Kress and van Leeuwen (2006) have shown, the visual has its own grammar and syntax comparable to, though not the same as, that of language. Image-makers, like writers, use their knowledge of the systemic resources of the visual, including principles of design and composition, to construct artful representations and convey their meaning as aptly as possible using the resources at their disposal. Clearly, they cannot determine a viewer's response but they can work to cue that response by positioning the viewer in particular ways (e.g. by creating social distance or by encouraging involvement and interactivity). What is excluded from a composition can be as significant as what is included, as we have seen in the case of Seawright who constructs a poetics of absence around the landscapes he photographs in war-torn Afghanistan.

That stories can be told pictorially rather than verbally has long been evidenced by religious art and representations of biblical stories in churches and chapels all over Europe and beyond. In this sense, the visual mode has a long history and it is legitimate to wonder what discussion of Seawright's war photographs can bring to notions of intermodal translation and a discussion of tendencies and developments in contemporary narrative where visual and verbal resources may be drawn on in storytelling. One answer relates back to notions of temporality and spatiality in narrative. What we have seen in relation to the visual mode is its dependency on context and culture, as well as on the ways, both material and critical, in which it engages with notions of time and space.

For as we have seen, Seawright's pictures constitute a series of 'takes' on a landscape and its history over time. There are recurrent themes and motifs and although the viewing order is not prescribed, we nevertheless 'read' the photographs which constitute the exhibition in (both prospective and retro-spective) relation to one another. Temporality also suffuses the images insofar as the past is recalled through images of the present which actively seek to evoke particular qualities (wistfulness, malevolence, menace, even timelessness) and to present aspects of reality which are not discrete and self-contained but form part of a larger (historical and psycho-geographical) picture. In terms of spatiality, it is not just what the viewer sees on the surface which is important but what that surface indexes about what lies below the surface or beyond the horizon.

In some ways, Seawright and Sebald are preoccupied with similar things: with the question of the limits of representation and of how to represent the ineffable, how to deal with conflict and trauma and how to uncover that which has remained hidden or which fails to disclose itself. When conventional narrative resources (be they visual or verbal) seem inadequate to the representational task at hand, writers and artists look for alternative means of achieving their aims or seek to extend the possibilities of their craft by importing ideas from other areas. Seawright's preoccupation is with what remains hidden from view and finding the visual means to express absence; Sebald's concern centres on 'a present reality shaped by [. . .] buried history' (Sebald 2006, p. 90) and 'an attempt to write a literary account of collective catastrophes' (p. 89) in the face of the seeming inability of writers to 'break out of the novel form that owes its allegiance to bourgeois concepts' (p. 89).

What Sebald is suggesting is that the novel form has been tied to an ideology which is no longer appropriate to the 'realities' of our world, a world which has seen massive conflicts and collective destructive urges. Neither historiographical methods nor 'pure' fiction are adequate to the task of representing 'a critical dialectic between past and present' (p. 99) which 'can lead to a learning process [. . .] not fated in advance to come to a "mortal conclusion"' (p. 99). This may help to explain Sebald's 'mixed' methods in creating a work which seems to defy easy generic categorization. He never saw himself as a novelist, yet he has left a literary legacy of the first order through his ability to construct a compelling account of the destructive effects of history on the life of his character Jacques Austerlitz. The blending of fact and fiction, the linking of an accumulation of descriptive detail and modes of philosophical enquiry, the incorporation of the visual and verbal in articulating a story all serve to make of *Austerlitz* a work which departs from convention and offers to writers the possibility of following a different narrative path.

Signal to Noise

I have been arguing that one of the predominant features of narrative today is its ability to draw on and combine visual and verbal modes. In the present chapter the focus so far has been on Sebald's *Austerlitz*, a work which harnesses the power of the visual in the service of a written narrative, at the same time as it employs visual modality to interrogate the limits of the word and of language. Likewise, Seawright's *Hidden* is a photographic record of images of Afghanistan which call attention to what is not seen on the surface, indexing instead what lies beyond the reach of the camera or outside its grasp. In this sense, the visual flags up its own representational limitations, even as it attempts to 'speak' of what it does not and cannot show.

In Neil Gaiman and Dave McKean's collaboration, *Signal to Noise* (2007), writer and graphic artist work together to translate their vision into a narrative which embodies the mutual dependency of visual and verbal modes. The story revolves around a film-maker who discovers he is dying just as he is about to embark on the production of a new film. Unsettled by news of his terminal illness, he decides to halt production and withdraws from the world, only to spend his time imagining the film he would have made. Eventually, he is compelled to write down what he sees in his mind's eye and leaves a copy for his producer after his death. The space of the film-maker's mind becomes, therefore, the site of a new production which is artfully realized within the pages of Gaiman and McKean's book.

The narrative is divided into 11 episodes, from 'Prelude' to 'Millennium' beginning with an interview with the film-maker and ending with a retrospective of his films filtered through the consciousness of his producer who clearly misses him. Across the chapters, the different strands of the story proceed in a largely linear way through a focus on the film-maker's last few months and his obsession with the film unfolding before him. There is a self-reflexive quality to the narrative in that the film-maker is making a film about millennialism and the question of the finitude of human existence at a time when he is very conscious of his own mortality and experiences a sense that time is coming to an end for him, even if it continues to mark the lives of others. As he imagines the village in central Europe where the film in his head is set, he thinks about the ticking of the clock as midnight approaches at the end of the first millennium in AD999: 'behind it I hear the echoes of other clocks [. . .] behind the ticking, behind the sound, I can hear the other: clean, sterile and cold [. . .]. I can hear the silence. And it won't go away' (chapter 6). Here, time is connected to mortality and silence to death, as the film-maker contemplates his own end.

Sight, including foresight or prescience, and vision are thematized across the various chapters. They are shown to be subject to impairment, not just physical but also psychological and emotional. Ability to project images onto the screen of our minds may depend as much on our capacity to remember as on the strength of our imaginations. People step out of the shadows and take centre stage; memories are lost or retained. The film-maker's mind is populated with images collected over time: faces he sees in a crowd which he then uses to create his inner cinema; or faces on photographs pinned to the wall of his study, what he calls '[a] patchwork of the nameless and the ones that interested me' (chapter 3). But looking can be a threatening act: when the film-maker looks at the photographs on the wall of his study, he feels as if they are looking back at him and shouts at them to stop.

Sound, white noise, and the degree of interference preventing reception of a signal is also thematized in the book. The title, *Signal to Noise*, reflects this preoccupation, as do aspects of the storyline and their visual realization. When the film-maker tells Inanna, his producer, that he's dying, she tries to reassure him by saying the usual kind of consolatory things but for the film-maker, it's '[j]ust noise' (chapter 3). In the film which he imagines, he sees a group of flagellants making noise as they whip themselves. A man with a baby asks them to be quiet but instead one of them redoubles his efforts and screams all the more loudly. A drunk sings and the film-maker comments on the noise and why people who believe that their world is coming to an end should continue making noise and living just as they have always done. Why, indeed, should he want to make a film that no one will see, he asks himself and answers his own question with the line: 'The world is always ending for someone' (chapter 5).

In addition to the parallel and intersecting storylines, there is a resonance or echo at the level of the progression of images. For example, the shadows of the tumour on the X-rays shown to the film-maker by his doctor cohere materially and associatively with the snowy blur which fills the frame or panel as he imagines bad weather interfering with the viewer's ability to see what is happening (chapter 1). In the aftermath of the discovery that he has a tumour, he glances at the lines on his palm as if to read his fate. In a series of panels (chapter 2) which move from mimetic to abstract, the lines on his hand are replaced by a 'network of grooves and trails' (chapter 2), then black and white patterings, and finally they dissolve into nothingness – the final panel is completely black. Likewise, the grainy quality of a photograph is seen to resemble the flickering of an empty TV screen (chapter 6).

These visual links help to bring otherwise potentially disparate elements together and create a network of associative meanings which underpin the work. That *Signal to Noise* is concerned with the construction of meaning is reflected in the quote from Barthes reproduced on the double title page: 'Everything has a meaning or nothing has. To put it another way, one could say that art is without noise.' At the level of the storyline, the film-maker's imminent death acts as an eventual spur to work on a film which itself thematizes questions of mortality and the purpose and nature of existence. What the reader witnesses is the film-maker's process, both his artistic process as he assembles images and constructs a storyline in his head and the process by which he comes to terms with his own mortality. The fact that he doesn't have much time left means that he wishes to fill it with something worthwhile – he wants to foreground the essential and relegate distractions to the background. Only when he is tired does he watch TV and the repetition of the adverts which become 'a mantra, a refrain, singing images held in time' (chapter 1).

For the film-maker's inner cinema to become the basis for a commercial or public production, he has to commit his ideas, images and voice to paper. This is what he passes on to Inanna so that she can help realize his artistic vision by making the film according to his specifications. But she cannot guard against others taking liberties with his legacy or adapting his work in ways she deems unsuitable. In that sense, while the dead may live on through their works, they are still in the hands of the living.

This somewhat cursory examination of *Signal to Noise* was intended to provide an example of a narrative that relies on both visual and verbal storytelling conventions and which manages to integrate them. It also serves to demonstrate the difference between a work such as that by Sebald which incorporates visual elements into its unfolding written narrative and a graphic novel such as that produced by Gaiman and McKean where the visual and verbal must work together to progress the story, notwithstanding the fact that this is a collaboration between a writer and graphic artist, rather than a work assured by a single individual. While arguably the rise of the graphic novel is a consequence of contemporary interest in the affordances of the visual and its ability to interact with the verbal, in terms of speech and thought representation, as well as in terms of sequencing and narrative progression, my interest in this chapter has been focused on the consequences for a dominant written narrative tradition of importing the visual. It has also been concerned to explore the specificities and disjunctions of the visual and verbal modes rather than examine their integration.

Concluding Remarks

In the introductory chapter, I suggested that narratives can be realized both visually and verbally and indeed by virtue of their interaction. Furthermore, I argued that the inclusion of the visual mode in verbal narratives represents a significant development in the shaping and elaboration of narratives today. As a consequence of the availability of technologies of communication, such development might appear a 'natural' step; however, the cultural signification of such forms of narrative meaning-making are not immediately transparent and necessitate examination. In focusing the present chapter predominantly on Sebald's *Austerlitz*, I have tried to show the various ways in which the visual and verbal modes can co-exist and interact to advance a storyline.

As we have seen, there is no one model: images can serve a variety of functions in relation to the verbal text which surrounds or accompanies it. With respect to *Austerlitz* my argument has been that what is at issue is a particular time-space configuration whereby the temporal is spatialized and the spatial is given a temporal dimension. The assumption of the dominance of time in narrative, in terms of progression, as well as in relation to the experiencing of events, actions and behaviours, is undercut by a disruption, even a suspension, of time. The spatial, which has always been part of narrative in metaphoric and imaginative terms, begins to be given literal extension. For narrative has always required a setting in which the action takes place and is presented from a particular perspective or set of perspectives. Moreover, the reader shifts from the world of actuality to the storyworld in the course of his/her encounter with the text before him/her in response to particular cues.

The development in *Austerlitz* lies in a particular conjunction and extension of philosophical and experiential issues: the relation of what we see to what we know and to what we feel; the place of semiotic systems, including language, in our intellectual and affective development; the role of memory in shaping present perceptions. These somewhat abstract sets of relations are explored in the context of the story of an individual – Jacques Austerlitz – set against the backdrop of a slice of European history, the awful reality of which has given cause for a re-assessment of notions of progress and ideas about human nature.

Austerlitz takes some of the apparent binaries explored in the introductory chapter (e.g. story/plot; story/discourse; history/fiction; time/space; mimesis/

diegesis) and subverts their status as oppositional elements. It re-configures ideas about 'storying' existence and about the prevalence or dominance of certain types of discourse in narrative and the exclusion of others (e.g. through the role of philosophical and academic discourse). Sebald takes implied oppositions (e.g. the language of fiction vs. the language of fact or 'subjectivity' vs. 'objectivity'; history vs. literature) and uses them in the service of creating a new form, one better suited to the times. In addition, he shows visual and verbal modes to be co-dependent in the context of the unfolding narrative. The visual has a role to play, as does the verbal but neither can exist on its own without loss of understanding of the texture and dynamics of the narrative as a whole.

Clearly, Sebald is not alone in using the affordances of visual and verbal modes to good effect. Advertising, for example, depends upon their functional specialization and interaction and the comic strip has long used representations of speech and thought in a series of visual frames to advance a storyline or set of ongoing episodes. In addition, as has been shown, the graphic novel is employing the conventions of both storytelling and cinema in innovative ways. In *Signal to Noise*, for example, the inclusion of a meta-narrative dimension and concern with processes of meaning-making served to illustrate the literary and philosophical potential of the graphic novel. What, perhaps, distinguishes Sebald's work is his breaking open of the novel form in the production of a new kind of narrative which seeks to reframe and reconstitute relations between the world of actuality with its events, actions and motivating behaviours and the world as presented in storied form. That he has chosen to do this by incorporating visual elements, originating from diverse sources into what is still a predominantly verbal narrative, is significant. This is a book imbued with the currents of history and haunted by the spectre of total destruction. Yet at its heart is an attempt to present one man's quest to come to terms with the hidden realities of his existence and to create a thick description of his situation and the social and historical networks of which he is a part and which have helped to constitute him.

Chapter 3

Intermedial Translation: Narrative across Media

Introduction

In *The Translation Zone: A New Comparative Literature*, Emily Apter (2006) sets out what she sees as relevant parameters for rethinking translation post-9/11 in an era of concern with conflict and communication; plurilingualism and creolization alongside English as a *lingua franca*; and technologies of communication which are 'increasingly challenging the boundaries of what translation is' (p. 10). Starting with a re-reading of Benjamin's 'The Task of the Translator' in conjunction with a number of his other pieces, including 'The Work of Art in the Era of its Reproducibility', she proposes a broad view of translation 'as an all-purpose, intermedial technology' (p. 7), characterizing it as 'the name for the ways in which the humanities negotiates past and future technologies of communication, while shifting the parameters by which language itself is culturally and politically transformed' (p. 11). What is of particular interest in the context of the current chapter is less the scope of the translational project as articulated by Apter (2006) than the designation of translation as intermedial technology. Certainly, the broad conception of translation inscribed and developed in the course of this book in relation to contemporary narrative/s is lent further support. However, given that the present chapter aims to focus on what is involved in moving or constructing narrative across media, as well as on the effects of medium on narrativity, the notion of translation as intermedial technology serves a number of functions.

First, it is a reminder of the mediated nature of *all* communicative practices, including translation and storytelling. Second, it points to the importance of understanding how developments in technologies of communication impact upon the re-production and re-creation of texts and artefacts. Thirdly, it brings to the fore a focus on process, as well as production, insofar as translation of a source text (ST) into a target text (TT) is seen to involve the negotiation of different cultural and linguistic topographies which, while they may overlap, do not map directly onto one another and cannot be reduced to a set of one-to-one correspondences. Rather there is recognition in Apter (2006) of translation as moving through one language into another through a continuum of transformations, thereby creating a zone which belongs to 'no single, discrete language or single medium of communication' (p. 6). From this perspective, translation is a process of adaptation and transformation with languages in dialogue across media.

Apter's focus is on what is involved in the process of translation from one language into another and with technologies of translation rather than on what happens in the process of adapting one kind of text into another, for example a novel into a screenplay. However, given the broad context in which she sets translation in relation to larger communicational and social processes, it is not incompatible with the view of textual adaptation to be articulated here. Indeed, Apter's acknowledgement of the potential impact on text production of the technologies mediating translation is very much in line with the position taken by social semioticians (e.g. Kress) and narratologists (e.g. Ryan) who point to the shaping influence of choice of medium on text.

The terminology can, however, be slippery, since words like 'mode' and 'medium' are not always used consistently. So it may be useful to review some of the key terms on which we shall draw in the present chapter and elaborate some working definitions.

Key Terms and Terminological Issues

As indicated above, I am using *translation* in a broad rather than narrow sense to refer to a process of textual production which depends on the existence of a prior or source text. Whether this text be in the same or in a different language to that produced as a result of engagement with the pre-existing text is not the determining factor here; rather, a broad conception of translation aims to include any text produced on the basis of another text. This 'originary' or source text may of course itself depend on other texts in a chain of (inter-) textual production. To a certain extent, it can be argued that all texts have relations of dependency on previous texts and that to a greater or lesser extent all texts are in fact intertextual. While not wishing to deny the logic of such a position, I wish to point here to explicit relations of dependency as is the case, for example, when a writer adapts a novel for the screen.

The word *text* itself requires perhaps a brief definition. By text, I understand, following Kress (2003), 'message entities' (p. 47) realized through a variety of means, including speech, image and writing. For Kress (2003, p. 48) text refers to 'any instance of communication in any mode or any combination of modes, whether recorded or not'. By *mode* is meant the means by which the communication is inscribed whether this be visually or verbally or both. Furthermore, Kress (2003, p. 45) divides mode into time-based (e.g. speech, dance) and space-based modes (e.g. image, sculpture) and indicates how their different logics – a temporal and a spatial logic respectively – underpin 'preferred textual/generic forms: *narrative* in speech and writing, and *display* in visual modes'.

As we will see in the course of this chapter, narrative as a time-based mode with an emphasis on (the relation of) events in sequence will be challenged by writers such as Virginia Woolf whose experimental fiction sought to disrupt narrative flow and create new sets of relations between and among the different dimensions of narrative text in terms of linearity, causality, thematic structure and coherence. Woolf's contribution to fiction can be seen as extending the spatial (and visual) possibilities of narrative text and placing temporal unfolding at the service of an apprehension of 'simultaneously present significant elements' (Kress, 2003, p. 45), to quote from Kress's characterization of spatial logic.

Medium relates to the site of appearance of the mode or modes (Kress, 2003, p. 48), whether on the page or on the screen. Kress (2003) argues that the new media of information and communication allow for greater facility in the combining of different modes and potentially permit greater interactivity than was possible in the past with respect to 'the older media of book and page' (p. 49). He is quick to point out, however, that the availability of technology in and of itself is not responsible for or driving the change but that 'the technological facility coincides with social, cultural, economic and political changes, all of which together are producing and pushing that change' (p. 49).

Where terminological difficulties may arise is in respect of language itself. Is language a medium which can be realized in the written or the spoken mode or is language a mode of communication with the medium through which it is realized, air in the case of spoken language and either the page or the screen in the case of written language? As we will see, for Ryan (2003) medium is a term likely to be differently understood depending on disciplinary base (e.g. sociology or philosophy) or professional domain (e.g. artist or art critic). Nevertheless, insofar as language has a substance and materiality and can be seen as a means of enabling (the realization of) artistic expression, it can be considered to fit Ryan's second, semiotic definition of medium, that is '[m]aterial or technical means of artistic expression' (Ryan, 2003, p. 2).

With these terminological differences in mind, let us turn now to three case studies which will attempt to flesh out the notion of intermedial translation, introduced above, and examine in more detail what takes place in the process of moving narrative across media, including the new media of information and communication. For as Kress (2003, p. 48) reminds us: 'The *screen* is the currently dominant site of appearance of text, but the screen is the site which is organized by the logic of image' (italics in original). The context in which Kress's remarks are made make clear that what he is discussing relates to literacy practices in the new media age (Kress, 2003) and that the screen to which he is referring is principally the computer screen. However, the logic of his argument and the general theoretical principles which underpin this alongside his other work on modes and media of contemporary communication (e.g. Kress and van Leeuwen, 2001) permit a broader construction of communicational practices in relation to media to include the big screen as well as the television screen. In what follows, the focus will be on the effects of choice of medium on narrativity as well as on the various transformations and translations entailed by the process of adaptation from one medium to another.

From Page to Screen: Case Study 1

The move from page to screen, with all that it entails, is one with which the late Anthony Minghella was very familiar. As a 'writer who directs' (Bricknell, 2005, p. 10), Minghella experienced at first hand what was involved in moving from the medium of the printed book to the medium of the screen, of translating a narrative written for the page into a credible film narrative. His thoughts and observations on this transpositional process, delivered in the context of interviews, newspaper articles and introductions to his screenplays, reflect his awareness of the affordances (Kress, 2003) of the different media as well as of the preferred modes of engagement likely to be triggered by them in the reading public or cinema-going audience. Thus, for Minghella, 'much of the pleasure in reading a novel is the creating of an inner landscape in which the book plays out, with each reader providing face and voice to a character, dramatizing events in the mind's eye, placing emphasis and finding in memory visual correlatives for scenes set in places beyond our experience' (Bricknell, 2005, p. 27). This personal and private cinema somehow has to be translated first into a screenplay, which Minghella characterizes as 'closer to an architect's drawing than it is to literature' (Bricknell, 2005, p. 29), and then, on the basis of this 'blueprint' (Bricknell, 2005, p. 29), made into a film. In referring to a screenplay as a blueprint, Minghella is also drawing attention to its potentially schematic properties in relation to the eventual film.

While this series of moves from the imagined or visualized to the visually realized may sound like a semi-continuous and interdependent process, what emerges from Minghella's attempts to describe it is a sense of the powerful effects of difference – different media, different purposes, different conventions and expectations – on both the construction and reception of the narrative/s produced. In referring to the process of adaptation in relation to his work as both screenwriter and director, Minghella points specifically to the differing requirements of the novel and the screenplay and addresses the different logics of the cinema and of prose fiction. For example, what he calls the 'metonymical quality of prose fiction gives way to the literal in films' (Bricknell, 2005, p. 29). By this he means to point to the fact that while language can evoke a scene or landscape or index a period by, for example, referring to typical aspects or items, the film needs literally to show them. Use of the word 'wireless', in preference to the word 'radio' for example may help to situate a novel in the 1940s. What it cannot do is to present to the reader a particular wireless, though s/he may well construct in imagination a prototypical image of a wireless on the basis of his/her prior exposure to wirelesses (or images thereof).

Likewise, according to Minghella, 'one of the problems of film is that you cannot handle tenses very well' (Bricknell, 2005, p. 15). The writer can indicate a character's endurance of a situation or phenomenon over time by simply stating it or s/he can indicate the passage of time by means of a temporal adjunct. The example given by Minghella is instructive:

> If I were writing the novel [*Cold Mountain*] I could say, 'For four years Inman had fought with the best of them; he killed more men and finally he had had enough'. That is a sentence which is almost impossible to achieve in a movie. (Bricknell, 2005, p. 15)

He goes on to indicate how he resolved through cinematographic means the problem of showing Inman to be a courageous combatant in the American Civil War who simply and understandably reaches a point of having had his fill of death and destruction and so decides to desert. What Minghella elects to do is to create, in the first ten minutes, 'quite a complex choreography in which you see the randomness of killing, you see Inman's exhaustion – and then you see him take his wound after the main battle because I wanted to show the irony that so many people got injured outside of the main conflicts' (Bricknell, 2005, p. 16).

The overarching point is that film and prose fiction employ different methods and techniques to create narrative and that these methods and techniques relate to differences in mode (e.g. written or spoken language; the presence or absence of the visual and/or the acoustic) and the materiality of the medium. Notwithstanding the oft-quoted mantra of 'showing' not 'telling' in fiction, it is clear that story as it is sequenced and conveyed through language requires different skills than those required to deliver a film narrative. The very fact of showing a wireless or a battle on screen, while not dictating the manner of presentation nor the function of the objects within the (edited) sequence of images demands a degree of specificity and concreteness atypical of prose where the word or stretch of text may point to or evoke in the reader an image or set of images without necessarily 'colouring them in' or making them fully determinate. As Kress (2003, p. 3) puts it: 'It is that "filling with meaning" which constitutes the work of imagination that we do with language.'

Conversely, in addressing the question of the means whereby cinema is able to achieve poetic or novelistic effects, Minghella points to the different mechanisms of the cinematographic medium and how they may be exploited:

> The cinema can manage its own poetry. Often this is achieved by manipulating the grammar of film, where shot size, camera angle and movement, the length of a shot, the amount of light on a subject, the palette of colours, and most significantly, the edit replace the syntax of noun, verb and adjective. (Bricknell, 2005, p. 30)

For Minghella, then, both film and prose fiction have their own affordances, constraints and logics. Specifically, they have their own 'grammars' which structure and regulate what is 'written' or produced and 'read' or consumed. Ultimately, for Minghella, film depends on 'visual rhyme and not narrative rhyme' (Bricknell, 2005, p. 35). What the characters say may, therefore, be less important than what is communicated through the juxtaposition of images in sequence.

The ability of a series of carefully edited moving images to 'speak volumes' is evidenced in the opening chapter of *The Talented Mr. Ripley*. One of the issues that Minghella had to tackle was how to provide a motivation for Ripley's behaviour and how to contextualize the series of events yet to unfold. Unlike the Patricia Highsmith novel where Ripley's killing of Dickie Greenleaf is premeditated, the Minghella adaptation focuses on the consequences for the character of what he calls the 'accumulation of one mistake' (Bricknell, 2005, p. 37) and presents a scene on the boat in San Remo where Dickie's murder seems both plausible and comprehensible – an argument that gets out of hand, vicious words, a blow in anger and one in self-defence before a fight to the death.

Right from the outset, as the credits are rolling, the juxtaposition of images serves to establish a sense of period and to create a kind of emotional and social geography, to echo Minghella's terms. The viewer sees the kind of life Tom Ripley is leading in New York and quickly understands his frustrations and aspirations. This is realized visually through the contrast between Tom's living and working conditions and the world into which he seeks entrance. It is his donning of a Princeton blazer and his decision to pretend acquaintance with Herbert Greenleaf's son, Dickie, which seems to have given him access to a world from which he is otherwise excluded.

Minghella is clearly aware of the importance of providing a context and set of characters as quickly as possible, if the viewer is to be drawn in to the story, and of the problem of realizing this visually:

> There are many jobs that have to be done at the beginning of a film. You have to know the period, you have to know the place, you have to know the circumstances and you have to know who the central character is – who you are supposed to be paying attention to – as quickly as possible. (Bricknell, 2005, p. 15)

The setting up of a dramatic situation and the introduction of the main character is achieved swiftly in the film's opening sequences by means of a prolepsis or flashforward, whereby we start with a scene chronologically situated at the end of the linear sequence of events, before returning to the moment that initiated the drama of whose tragic end we get a preview. So the film cuts from a focus on Ripley's forlorn and desolate face, as he sits in the interior of a cabin, to an open-air recital in central New York at which Ripley is accompanying a young soprano on the piano. In relation to the function of such a prolepsis in fiction, Herman (2002, p. 217) points out that 'proleptic storytelling, by eliminating or reducing narrative suspense, requires an interpretive reori- entation on the part of readers' which prompts them to focus on the how and why of events, rather than on the events themselves. In the context of the film version of *The Talented Mr. Ripley*, we can see it as a way of encouraging the viewer to think about what led up to this moment of desolation and regret on Ripley's part and what might have motivated Ripley to behave as he has done.

The opening sequence also serves Minghella's need to provide a context for Ripley's actions that would allow evidence of motivation to emerge. We are invited to place Ripley in a social, psychological and cultural landscape and to construct his journey from 'a real nobody' in New York to 'a fake somebody' in Italy (Minghella, 2000, p. x), and from 'the borrowing of a jacket [. . .] [to] the borrowing of an identity' (p. xi). As viewers, we register Ripley's belated desire for things to have been otherwise and hear (off-stage) his note of regret: 'If I could just go back. If I could rub everything out. Starting with myself. Starting with borrowing a jacket' (Minghella, 2000, p. 1). For Minghella (2000, p. x), it is '[f]ilm grammar, with its unique ability to manipulate images, flexing from the intense close-up to the broadest vistas, [which] is perfectly placed to situate personal behaviour in a public landscape'. In other words, he is keenly aware of the role played by the choice of medium on the construction and delivery of the narrative and of the need to take account of its possibilities and limitations.

Minghella's views, as both a writer and director, seem to chime with the work of narrative theorists such as Ryan who are concerned with the 'configuring action of the medium' (Ryan, 2003, p. 3) and its shaping effects on narrative presentation. In line with Herman (2002, p. 214) for whom the 'mode of telling also bears crucially on – indeed, alters – the matter told', Ryan's interest is in looking systematically at the impact of medium, in the dual sense of channel of communication and means of artistic expression, on the type of story told. In other words, she emphasizes both the transmissive and semiotic dimensions of medium and points to the potential of a material support to shape the manner in which the 'message' or information is received. Ryan's definition of narrative makes clear that she does not equate narrative with a particular type of written text but as:

a mental image, or cognitive construct, which can be activated by various types of signs. This image consists of a world (*setting*) populated by intelligent agents (*characters*). These agents participate in *actions and happenings* (events, plot), which cause global *changes* in the narrative world. Narrative is thus a mental representation of causally connected states and events which captures a segment in the history of a world and of its members. (Ryan, 2003, pp. 1–2; italics in original)

What is of importance here is first Ryan's recognition of narrative as a dynamic construct capable of realization across media. At the same time, attention is drawn to the fact that technologies of communication and modes of expression can interact in ways which support distinct types of narrativity. So, for example, Ryan (2003, p. 4) points to the dependence of daily newspapers on a 24-hour news cycle which impacts upon coverage of news stories as a result of which they 'lack the completeness and retrospective perspective of other types of narrative'. Clearly the manner of presentation of worlds populated by actors engaging in actions, the consequences of which result in some kind of change within the narrative world, is not just a factor of individual difference but also a factor of mode (e.g. written or spoken), medium (e.g. print medium or screen) and the conventions of the genre (e.g. comedy or tragedy).

As we have seen in the case of Minghella as he moved from Patricia Highsmith's novel experienced as entering 'an airless, claustrophobic world with Tom Ripley' (Minghella, 2000, p. viii) to the film via the screenplay which he holds to be 'both an argument with the source material and a commentary on it' (p. ix), moving from one medium to another is facilitated by an awareness of the narrative possibilities of each and of the likely consequences of the story's transposition from one context to another. What is also of interest given the contention made with respect to the notion of intermedial translation and the continua of textual transformations likely to result from such an engagement is Minghella's reference to the source material as point of departure in a dialogic process of argument and commentary. Minghella is clearly recognizing the interpretative, critical and creative dimensions of text production within a translational context.

From Page to Stage: Case Study 2

Such concerns with narrative transposition are also reflected in the move from page to stage effected by Katie Mitchell and her company in *Waves*, a multimedia production devised on the basis of Virginia Woolf's experimental novel, *The Waves*, first published in 1931. Mitchell has long been interested both in Woolf – she studied English Literature at Oxford and did a special paper on Woolf – and in finding a 'language' appropriate to contemporary theatre. In an interview with Christopher Campbell at the National Theatre (12 January 2007), she indicated the motivation for choosing *The Waves* citing it as the challenge of solving a problem, since in her view it is formally the most difficult of Woolf's novels and the one likely to be most difficult to stage.

This challenge can be attributed to a number of things: the nature of *The Waves* itself insofar as it is a poetic and largely 'plotless' novel in a conventional sense; the effect of 'translating' the novel for the stage and moving from a temporal medium with one channel (the linguistic) to a spatio-temporal medium with multiple channels (linguistic-acoustic-visual), to draw on Ryan's (2003, p. 6) typology; and Mitchell's express desire to extend the range of possibilities in mainstream theatre (cf. Shevtsova, 2006). Of course, these aspects of what is involved in the process of adaptation are not discrete but tend to interact and impact dynamically on the shape of the final production. In other words, the move from page to stage is the product of a set of operations (analytic, cognitive, creative and expressive), performed both individually and in collaboration, which are constrained by the materiality of the medium and can be situated in relation to social, cultural and discourse practices.

Such an account of intermedial translation may appear to factor out elements of chance and serendipity which are likely to be part and parcel of the 'creative' process of adaptation of an experimental novel into a multimedia stage production involving a degree of trial and error and improvisation. However, while it would be wrong to reduce the complexities of what Mitchell (Campbell, 2007) describes as a search 'for the most exquisite way of executing the ideas that the words have given you' to a set of rational and methodical steps, it is interesting to note that the language she uses to discuss her working practices in general reflects a high degree of awareness and self-reflection. In addition, she seems to reject the notion of artistic vision but sees it rather as a series of small, concrete components that build up into what other people (e.g. critics; other artists) may formulate in such terms or refer to as the Katie Mitchell 'method'.

For Mitchell (Campbell, 2007), the interest or the challenge, as she would have it, lies in capturing human behaviour using tools appropriate to the medium and to the topic. At the same time, she appears committed to pushing the boundaries of mainstream theatre and importing into it insights, techniques and practices from other domains, such as the visual arts, dance and avant-garde theatre. As is the case with Minghella whose practices as a writer and film director are informed by his experience of other areas (e.g. theatre and scriptwriting for television as well as a long-standing interest in music), Mitchell's background in theatre is coloured by an interest in film, dance and the visual arts. For example, she points to the long-lasting influence on her of 'the combination of subtle acting with poetic images' (Shevtsova, 2006, p. 5) of the films of Tarkovski. She also mentions the formative influence of an interest in neuroscience and psychology which has helped to shape her approach to theatre insofar as she likes to focus on the triggering of (primary and social) emotions through movement and gesture rather than necessarily through language. She also sees sound as a powerful trigger, describing it, in the context of a discussion of *Iphigenia at Aulis*, as 'another tool to work with on creating emotion in the audience and, therefore, communicating the idea of the play' (Shevtsova, 2006, p. 13). This interest in the effects of sound is evident also in *Waves* as are the results of Mitchell's study of Pina Bausch's work on video with its 'attention [. . .] to design, space and light' (Shevtsova, 2006, p. 17).

In short, what emerges in conversation with Mitchell is a sense of a theatre director whose 'method' combines analysis and research with improvisations and technical innovations. Her project to devise a multimedia work based on *The Waves* appears to have been motivated by her long-standing interest in Woolf and by the challenge of realizing the work, in collaboration with her company, in a different medium. In choosing *The Waves*, from among Woolf's novels, she was conscious of the challenges likely to arise in the process of adaptation, challenges related to and stemming from the differences in medium and likely to result in different types of narrativity. She viewed these challenges as a problem to be solved collaboratively, indicating that 60–70 per cent of the 'solutions' to the problem were generated by the company in rehearsal.

The book which provides a record of the multimedia work devised by Katie Mitchell and her company is composed of:

> images [. . .] that were output live to the projection screen during the performance. They were created on the stage beneath the projection screen by the ensemble using video cameras, lights, props and costumes [. . .]. The text is made up almost entirely of extracts from Virginia Woolf's novel, *The Waves*, written in 1931. There are also a few paragraphs from her book *Moments of Being* (Mitchell, 2008, p. 5).

In referring to the images projected onscreen by members of the cast, this extract gives some sense of the production as drama-in-the-making as well as pointing to its dependence on a combination of modes including the visual, the acoustic and the linguistic. While the book can capture in the form of static images and blocks of text a sequenced selection of some of the elements which combined to make up the performance, what it cannot do is re-present that performance in its entirety and in real time. This observation returns us in essence to the focus of the present chapter which aims to investigate what is involved in the process of translation from one medium to another and how and to what extent the (choice of) medium impacts upon narrativity. As Ryan (2003, p. 3) points out, what counts as a medium is 'a category that truly makes a difference as to what stories can be evoked or told, how they are presented, why they are communicated, and how they are experienced'. She goes on to indicate the three grammatical domains in which narrative differences can be found – semantics, syntax and pragmatics – and aligns them with corresponding areas in narrative theory, where 'semantics becomes the study of plot, or story; syntax becomes the study of discourse, or narrative tech-niques; and pragmatics, an area still relatively unfamiliar to literary critics, becomes the study of narrative as performance' (Ryan, 2003, p. 3).

While, as we have seen, it is important to differentiate story and plot, where the former relates to the linear sequence of events and the latter focuses on the motivation of a particular conjunction or configuration of events, Ryan's categorization of narrative domains appears to offer a way of accounting for the various levels of narrative transposition. In relation to Mitchell's multimedia production, therefore, the area of narrative pragmatics clearly comes to the fore inasmuch as we are dealing with a spatio-temporal medium – the stage – in which stories are told and dramas unfold in real time through a combination of the linguistic-acoustic-visual (kinetic) channels. Unless the whole performance is video-recorded, it is experienced as an ephemeral event. Just as the screen-play can be seen as a blueprint, to recall Minghella's words, for the eventual film, so the text of a play or script, can be seen as a kind of template or schematic structure which is brought to life in the actual production.

At the same time, it is important to remember the potentialities of the page, which can often be presented as a seemingly one-dimensional, static text rather than a dynamic, multimodal one. Yet, as Kress (2000, p. 186) has pointed out, language itself is a multimodal system which can be realized in written or spoken form. Writing may in turn be realized in different media, as marks on a page or inscriptions in metal, stone, canvas and so on, while spoken language can be transmitted through the air or airwaves or captured in electronic and digital form. In short, for Kress (2000, p. 187): 'Just as there are multiple modes involved in the production of any text, there are often multiple media.' He goes on to suggest that a culture's focus on particular modes and media at any given time has repercussions in terms of how people are permitted to engage with their world.

> Assuming that we, as biological and physiological beings, are not all equally disposed to the forms most developed by and valued by our cultures, some members of one culture will be less well served than others; some will be affectively and cognitively at an advantage over those others whose preferred sensory modes are not valued or are suppressed in their culture. (Kress, 2000, p. 187)

Kress is pointing here not only to the fact that our engagement with the world is socially, culturally and technologically mediated and circumscribed but also to the fact that differences in the value/s assigned by a culture to particular modes and media of communication may privilege certain groups or indi-viduals at any particular historical moment. At one level, then, access to modes and media of communication becomes a social and political issue and not just a question of preference. At the same time, the development of new communication technologies serves both to extend the possibilities of repres-entation and engagement with the world and to mediate our experience of it in non-trivial ways.

Mitchell's multimedia production of Woolf's *The Waves* is a case in point insofar as the range of tools and technologies employed by the company (video cameras, lights, props and costumes as well as materials for creating sound effects) enables the realization of an imaginational world at the same time as it points to the means of its construction and mediation through language, gesture, action, sound, colour and dance. It shows the process by which the novel has been 'staged' both in the sense of being adapted for the stage and being the product of a narrative staging.

As previously indicated, Mitchell's choice of *The Waves* was motivated. Her interest lay in taking what she describes in the interview as formally the hardest of Woolf's novels and the most difficult to stage. In considering why this might be the case, it is useful to return to the text of *The Waves* itself and to revisit it in relation to concepts of narrative and multimodality. As Flint (1992, p. ix) indicates: '*The Waves* (1931) presents a challenge to the reader' by virtue of the fact that Woolf was attempting to take fiction in a different direction from that pursued in the past. Bradbury (1989, p. 234) describes Woolf's distrust of 'the materialism and specificity of fictional realism of the Arnold Bennett kind' and her 'repudiation of the Edwardian novel'. Woolf herself famously rejected the techniques and tools of what she considered an outmoded realism and sought to find a form of the novel which would better express her concern with character and the interior lives, rather than the outward trappings, of her protagonists. *The Waves* posed 'a set of formal problems' (Flint, 1992: xviii) which she strove through the process of writing and rewriting to overcome. In other words, Woolf was conscious of the need to break from traditional notions of narrative which emphasized the sequential ordering of a series of events and the motivated transformation of participants over time. Instead she focused on poetic prose and claimed to be writing *The Waves* 'to a rhythm not a plot' (Flint, 1992, p. xxi).

Interestingly, this recalls Minghella's concern with 'visual rhyme and not narrative rhyme' (Bricknell, 2005, p. 35) in relation to the transposition of novel to film. While Woolf's comment does not relate to transposition in this sense, she is clearly conscious of shifting the focus of narrative interest away from (the relation of) external events and happenings, and their motivation, towards a concern with the inner lives of characters and a representation of their 'patterns of mind' in a language that seeks to reflect the rhythms of consciousness and inner speech (Flint, 1992, p. xxxvii). In other words, notions of causality and a focus on chronology are less important than conveying a sense of inner realities and subjective perceptions which may or may not cohere with the externals of existence. As Flint (1992, p. xxxvii) contends, '[t]his demand that we consider the subjectivity inherent in all expression, yet that we simultaneously acknowledge that language cannot control, cannot stabilize our sense of selfhood, is crucial to our understanding of *The Waves.*'

The mode of organization of *The Waves*, then, is such that the narrative flow is punctuated by an evocation of the sound and movement of the waves and a description of the positioning of the sun and the quality and intensity of the light as day breaks and dawn moves to dusk. Both the visual and the acoustic potentialities of language are brought to the fore: visual insofar as a scene of waves breaking against the shore is created through language; acoustic to the extent that the phrasing and the poetical prose serve to convey the motion of the waves. For example:

> As they neared the shore each bar rose, heaped itself, broke and swept a thin veil of white water across the sand. The wave paused, and then drew out again, sighing like a sleeper whose breath comes and goes unconsciously. (Woolf, 1992, p. 3)

The swelling of the waves and the slight hesitation before they break are rendered through the use of punctuation, length of clause, and through the prosody. Even if the text is not read aloud, the rhythm can be heard with the inner ear.

Kress's (2003) emphasis on the spatial potentials of the page, in contradistinction to the temporal ordering of speech as a time-based mode warrants further consideration here. For Kress (2003, p. 46), writing is a mixed mode insofar as it 'leans heavily still – in alphabetically recorded languages – on the temporality of speech but has begun to make use of spatial resources, both actually and virtually'. These spatial resources include spacing and paragraphing, indents and blocks of writing, as well as 'the hierarchical structures of the syntax of writing' (p. 46). In Woolf's novel, as has been discussed, the descriptions of the waves framing the sequences of what superficially appears to be dialogue reported by a narrator, serve to 'interrupt' the stretches of text recording the thoughts, anxieties and characteristic behaviours of the six characters – Bernard, Susan, Rhoda, Neville, Jinny and Louis – to whose inner lives the reader has access over a number of years from their days at nursery to a meeting at Hampton Court.

While at one level, there remains a biographical and chronological narrative in the sense that we see the characters at different points in their lives as those lives intersect, this linearity is challenged in a number of ways. First, the intercalation of the poetic passages describing the movement of the waves and the cyclical nature of time takes the reader out of one narrative mode into another. Second, the 'dialogues' turn out on closer inspection to be more like soliloquies or examples of inner speech masquerading as reported speech. 'The most personal thoughts, she [Woolf] suggests, may be most satisfactory when distanced through the formality of deliberated composition' (Flint, 1992, p. xxxvi). Third, there is a sense in which the stretches of 'dialogue' relating to particular temporal and spatial locations (e.g. the nursery, the school room, the restaurant) present a series of tableaux in which the characters are located relative to one another within that particular setting and, at the same time, across settings, individual characters are recognizable not just through the tag (e.g. Bernard said, Susan said) but also because their thoughts are recorded in language which reflects their recurring preoccupations over time. For example, Bernard's recurring preoccupation relates to storytelling and trying to capture the world or aspects thereof in a narrative which might serve to give it shape but life intervenes, the story is interrupted, the words are never quite adequate to the experience. The gap between inner and outer worlds, the solidity of the phrase and the fragility of the moment are mismatched.

> And, half-way through dinner, we felt enlarge itself round us, the huge blackness of what is outside us, of what we are not. The wind, the rush of wheels became the roar of time, and we rushed – where? And who were we? We were extinguished for a moment, went out like sparks in burnt paper and the blackness roared. Past time, past history we went. For me this lasts but one second. It is ended by my own pugnacity. I strike the table with a spoon. If I could measure things with compasses I would, but since my only measure is a phrase, I make phrases – I forget what on this occasion. (Woolf, 1992, p. 213)

If I have quoted this passage at length, it is because it brings together a number of interrelated themes essential to the novel as a whole: How to find a means of expression adequate to the job of representing the 'realities' of existence, means which may indeed conflict with conventional notions of novel-writing and require the creation of new forms for new times. How to catch hold of the moment which has already receded even as its importance or effect has just been grasped. When Bernard is confronted by the inadequacy of his own phrase-making, which fails to translate lived experience in all its complexity and ambiguity but which tapers out and is never complete, he is recognizing that the tools and conventions at his disposal are not up to the job. As Woolf (1992, p. 80) put it in relation to the Edwardian novelists whose method she so despised: 'But those tools are not our tools, and that business is not our business. For us, those conventions are ruin, those tools are death.'

As has been shown, Woolf helped to extend the possibilities of narrative through realizing its spatial potentialities, potentialities that the traditional nineteenth- century novel had perhaps overlooked in its quest for linearity and motivated progression through time. Katie Mitchell's multimedia 'adaptation' makes concrete and explicit this spatial dimension in the new medium. But it is not simply a question of transposition from page to stage, since clearly the stage itself can be differently organized. Her production serves to highlight what can be seen as an organizing principle of the novel, namely that it revolves around a series of meetings and partings (cf. Bakhtin's notion of the chrono-tope) realized in different locations at particular times in the lives of the characters. The rearranging of materials and items on stage to form the next scene and the shifting configurations of characters over time is enacted on stage such that a narrative unfolds in space rather than principally over time. Of course the production takes place in time and has duration, just as a novel is read in and over time. However, the space of the stage is changed by the actions performed upon it and by the 'stacking up' of scenes and indications of different time frames signalled by the writing of dates on a chalk board, dates which are immediately erased after having been written. Time is under erasure, it is physically wiped out. The trace which it leaves is visible only in the new configurations of actors on stage performing their roles as characters in a drama. The audience sees them donning their costumes and is exposed to the props they use to create the illusion of time passing, as well as to re-create the 'feel' of a particular time. Paradoxically, perhaps, the distancing effect which exposure to the means of production can create ultimately serves to draw the audience in to this 'virtual' world.

So far in this chapter we have examined the possibilities of narrative across media and have investigated what happens in the process of transposition across media in terms of effect upon narrativity and in relation to the affordances and constraints of the medium, that is, what it permits or licenses and the type/s of engagement with the world it may (or may not) afford. However, apart from brief consideration of the use of video in Katie Mitchell's *Waves*, it might appear that not much attention has been given to the 'new' media. In looking at the move from page to screen in terms of the 'big screen' or cinema, we saw what was involved in the process from the perspective of a writer-director, a writer-director in the case of Anthony Minghella, who is aware of what he is trying to achieve and is skilled in working with and within cinematographic parameters and particular generic conventions.

Clearly what was once a new spatio-temporal medium – cinema – is now well established. However, in terms of the technological resources that directors today have at their disposal and that can be harnessed to enable (or disrupt) storytelling and create special effects, cinema has in many ways changed from the era of black and white, silent movies. The point is not that technological advances lead to or necessarily mean 'better' storytelling but rather that the ways in which narrative is realized or instantiated across media is in part a factor of the capacities of those media and the ways in which particular modes and media interact. As technologies develop, possibilities for extending conceptions of narrative or realizing different aspects of narrative arise.

Evidence of this can be seen in online or digital narratives which use the affordances of technology to 'flesh out' the experience of entering or immersing oneself in another world and, in some cases, attempt to increase the degree of interactivity in the co-production/co-construction of the narrative. Of course, the activity of reading is itself interactive insofar as the reader is attempting to make meanings on the basis of graphic and visual cues. Using his/her knowledge of the world and drawing on experience of other possible worlds, the reader constructs from the words on the page a plausible storyworld, plausible, that is, in terms of the narrative frame and not necessarily in terms of what is possible in actuality (cf. Herman, 2002). However, in an online narrative, the reading pathways can be more complex with a combination of written text, visual images, some static, some dynamic, set against an acoustic backdrop (e.g. music and other sound effects).

I wish to turn now to an example not of an adapted text but to one designed and constructed specifically with the affordances of the new media in mind. The result of collaboration between a digital writer and a graphic artist, it sets out to access multiple modes and to help develop multiple literacies through the provision of a series of narrative episodes, some of which are still under construction, recounting the story of the main protagonist, Alice, as she develops over time and moves from one location to another.

Narrative and the New Media: Case Study 3

According to the description on the opening page, *Inanimate Alice*, written and designed by Kate Pullinger and Chris Joseph,

> tells the story of Alice, a young girl growing up in the first half of the 21st century, and her imaginary digital friend, Brad.
>
> Over ten episodes, each a self contained story, we see Alice grow from an eight year old living with her parents in a remote region of Northern China to a talented mid-twenties animator and designer with the biggest games company in the world. (Pullinger and Joseph, 2005, http://www. inanimatealice.com)

To date only four of the planned ten episodes are available. Of the four currently online, the different episodes become progressively longer and more interactive. By way of example, I shall focus on two episodes: the first and the third.

The initial episode is entitled 'China' and is billed as being the least interactive and lasts approximately 5 minutes. Clicking on arrows on the screen takes the viewer/reader from one page to the next, as the story unfolds. The basic storyline in this episode revolves around the disappearance of Alice's father, who makes trips in his jeep from the base camp in Northern China where they live, and their recovery of him several days later, after they decide to go out in search of him.

At one level the story is traditionally structured around a journey made in search of a missing person who is later recovered, that is it is a quest story with a happy ending. It is told from the child's perspective and uses relatively simple language, including the kinds of observations and distractions which might be typical of a young child on a long and difficult journey, albeit a twenty-first century child with a ba-xi player with a writing and drawing facility able to shoot and send photos. The narrative tension is created not just by the expressions of fear and anxiety on the part of the child and (indirectly) by her mother: 'She tells me to turn off my player, it's annoying her. She is frightened. I am frightened too. It's getting darker. The sky is humming.' It is rendered too by the music which pulsates through the narrative, keeping up the pressure until John, Alice's father, is spotted. The reunion is accompanied by different, less discordant, less frantic music with a Chinese flavour reflecting not just the location but also alluding to the fact that John's wife, Ming, is Chinese.

In addition, the images, both static (e.g. photos, maps, sectional drawings) and moving (e.g. a jeep traversing difficult, desert-like terrain) serve to create what is described in the online explanatory notes for teaching *Inanimate Alice* as a multisensory experience:

> 'Inanimate Alice' is easily assimilated into learning environments; its use of multimodality (images, sounds, text, interaction) enables students to see storytelling in a new, multi-sensory light. 'Inanimate Alice' is a new media fiction that allows students to develop multiple literacies (literary, cinematic, artistic, etc.) in combination with the highly collaborative and participatory nature of the online environment. (http://www.inanimatealice.com/education/index.html)

Notwithstanding the explicitly pedagogic agenda, it is clear that an attempt has been made in the realization of this digital narrative to combine aspects of literary and cinematographic narratives and extend them via the possibilities offered by the new medium. As Page (2008) puts it in her blog on digital narratives: '[. . .] *Inanimate Alice's* multiplicity extends beyond its use of semiotic resources, also exploiting the creative synergies between narratives in new media and computer gaming.' This conjunction of narrative and gaming is perhaps best exemplified by comparing the read-only versions with the game versions. With respect to episode three, which is set in Russia, the difference between versions resides in the fact that the game version requires the reader/player to collect the requisite number of dolls in order for the guard at the checkpoint to let Alice and her parents through. So as well as following Alice's adventures by clicking on the arrows, thereby progressing the narrative, it is necessary to play the game by manoeuvring to catch the Russian dolls which would otherwise crash to the ground.

As with episode one, the storyline is relatively straightforward and is told from Alice's perspective – she is now 13. She has had to hide in the closet while her parents argue with strange men who come to their house at night. She has been living in Russia with her father, John, and mother, Ming, for two years now and had hoped to join the International School but because of kidnappings, her father insists she continue to be educated at home. He works in the oil industry and there appears to have been some kind of leak or contamination, for which he seems to have been blamed. Eventually they decide to pack up and leave, taking very little with them. They make it through the first check point but are stopped at the second. In the read-only version, they are eventually waved through after the guard realizes that Alice's player is not an industrial espionage device or something that would compromise security. They manage to board a 'plane but Alice does not know where they are headed'.

While the storyline is not particularly novel, what is of interest is the way in which it is realized through the various modes and their interaction. Suspense is created right from the beginning as a rather dark silhouette of Moscow appears on the screen while music, which would not be out of place in a thriller or Cold War film, plays. Then the reader/viewer is shown a door opening onto a bedroom which appears to be empty. The text tells us that Alice is hiding in the closet; loud voices, presumably speaking in Russian, are heard in the background. The images of Moscow that accompany the text indicating that they have been living there for two years are monochromatic, dark and sinister and the apartment in which they live is described by Alice as 'old and decrepit and depressing'. Most of the action takes place at night and the screen is invariably dimly lit adding to the sense of both mystery and gloom.

As with film, the selection of images in digital narratives helps to create atmosphere and set the scene. However, it also constrains insofar as the reader is not free to imagine or 'colour in' the scene for him- or herself, as in verbal print narratives. The concept of linearity is also complicated by the reading path which must be taken. Since the reader progresses through the narrative by clicking on the arrow, sequence is a factor not of turning a page but of replacing one text-image combination by another. At the level of narrative sequence, there is still an attempt to 'connect' the various scenes presented to the reader, though at times, it's rather like 'show and tell': while, in episode three, Alice 'talks' about the International School and how cool she found the kids there, what look like Polaroid shots of various locations and activities appear on screen and fan out like a pack of cards.

Clearly, the kinds of links made here between text and image, as well as the type of reading path taken differ from what we might find in a (more or less) traditional print narrative. In the case of *Inanimate Alice* where the story is told by a young girl, the fact that the sentence structure is relatively simple and the number of words per page small is in tune with what might be expected of (in this case) a 13-year-old (e.g. 'I'm hiding in the big closet in my bedroom'; 'My room is large and has big, dirty windows'); however, in the case of a narrative related by an adult narrator reader expectations might be different in terms of the complexity and length of sentences.

The question of the affordances and constraints of the online environment in the design and production of digital narratives, as well as the relationship between text and image, presents itself, if digital narratives are to be more than simply text transposed to a digital medium. This would include concern with how much text readers can absorb, along with such questions as the size and colour of font, how 'busy' the screen appears etc. In other words, there is a physicality to the design of the online environment which must be taken into account in relation to the construction and progression of the narrative.

Additionally, in this case, there is the possibility of increasing the degree of interactivity by electing to play the game version. This is where gaming meets narrative, as Page indicated. By interactivity, I mean to point to haptic engagement on the part of the user with the tools designed to affect what happens in the narrative or which constrain choices in a particular way (e.g. the number of Russian dolls collected determines whether or not the guard allows Alice and her family to proceed). The concept of interactivity is complicated by the fact that there are system, as well as user, constraints. As Harrell and Zhu (2009, p. 47) put it:

> In digital environments, a user's power to take meaningful actions is mediated through the structure provided by the computational system as well as the socially situated interpretation of actions rendered by the user. A system's capacity to afford certain actions, impose certain constraints, and reward certain behaviors clearly has great effect on user's (sic) agency.

While their discussion largely relates to questions of agency in interactive narratives and gaming contexts, the general point regarding perceived and actual degree of freedom and ability to impact upon the story is nevertheless valid in respect of *Inanimate Alice*. For one of the possible differences in narratives which can be seen to be a consequence of the affordances of the medium is precisely this ability to interact physically and not just psychically with aspects of the storyworld. As Warren (2010, p. 41) indicates, *Inanimate Alice* is an 'example of a digital narrative that would not exist in the same way in printed form'.

The overarching point is that the type/s of narrativity which can be accessed and realized can be seen to depend not just on modes of textual organization (e.g. predominantly linear or predominantly spatial) but also on the very materiality and affordances of the chosen medium. Advances in computer software and the deployment of narrative resources in a multimodal environment onscreen have the potential to change the dynamics of storytelling. In other words, storytelling in the digital age is likely to be experienced differently than storytelling before the age of print, for example. This is not to suggest a progression from oral to written to digital narrative nor to privilege one set of tools or technologies over another. It is simply to situate developments in narrative in a sociocultural and technological context which may impact upon their production and reception in non-trivial ways. By non-trivial, I mean to point to the possible effects (e.g. cognitive, affective) of different modes of engagement with the world, following Kress (2003, p. 173).

> Introducing a concern with materiality and the senses into representation brings the long-standing separation in Western thinking of mind and body into severe question, and therefore challenges the reification and consequent separation of cognition, affect and emotion. It becomes untenable to assume that cognition is separable from affect; all representation is always affective, while it is also always cognitive.

It may be that the facilities of the new media enable this inseparability of the cognitive and affective to be newly recognized through concrete realization of the available mix of modes designed and produced by the digital writer and activated by the viewer/online reader. In other words, it is what Kress (2003, p. 49) calls 'the potentials for action by writers and readers, makers of texts and remakers of texts, the matter, so called, of interactivity', as well as 'the hugely greater facility for using a number of modes in the making of texts'. In clicking on the icons, following sets of instructions, playing games or solving problems, the outcome of which may have some bearing on the progression of the story, the sense of playing one's part in the construction of the narrative is given material extension.

In addition, the multimodal nature of many online narratives which are realized through the interaction of text, image and sound, can add to a sense of 'realism' or at least emphasize the (multi-)sensory nature of the experience. Sounds are heard, images, both moving and static, can be viewed, text can be read. From this perspective, the online or digital narrative can be seen as less skeletal, more fully realized and more determinate than the kind of print narrative which relies on language alone to cue and guide a reader's interpretation and visualization of the story, the setting and the characters. This relative openness or indeterminateness – 'that "filling with meaning" which constitutes the work of imagination that we do with language' (Kress, 2003, p. 3) – may well be qualitatively different to the kind of work we do in reading online narratives, just as watching a film is a different experience to reading a book.

Furthermore, if we consider Vygotsky's (1978) work on the development of higher psychological processes in relation to symbolic and sign systems, and cultural and technological tools, it can be argued that the role of tools in mediating and constructing interaction, as well as the dialogue around it, whether articulated or internalized, can affect cognition and patterns of mind. As Kress (2003, p. 22) puts it: 'A vast change is underway, with as yet unknowable consequences.'

Conclusion

We seem perhaps to have come a long way from narrative and concepts of narrativity across media but in effect what has remained in focus has been the contention discussed across the chapter that the ways in which narrative is realized depends on a dialogue between reader/viewer and writer/producer of text and that the tools and technologies which mediate and help to shape the product/ion impact upon their apperception and construction. The medium in which narrative is produced and the sociocultural conditions surrounding its 'use' will necessarily affect its production. From the point of view of the writer-director or theatre director translating narrative across media, it is important to understand what is involved in the process of transposition and adaptation, including the possibilities and limitations of the particular modes and media under consideration so as to be able to negotiate the meaning-making process more skilfully, artfully and creatively. Likewise, for the digital writer or animator, it is not just a question of technological facility and the ready availability of text, image and sound but of understanding what makes a 'good' story in particular environments and how this might successfully be 'plotted' online.

With respect to narrative and its potential to be realized across media, we have seen that moving from one medium to another is a kind of translation involving decision-making and negotiation in the light of considerations such as the affordances of mode and the facilities of media as well as in relation to the critical and creative scope of the translational project as imagined and realized by the writer-producer/re-maker of text and re-created by the reader/viewer/co-constructor of text.

Chapter 4

Intercultural Translation: Language and Culture as Narrative Resource

Introduction

In the preceding two chapters, the concept of translation in a broad sense has been employed to underpin discussion of what happens in the process of moving from one mode to another (e.g. visual to verbal) or from one medium to another (e.g. page to screen) with a view to stressing the dynamics of textual transposition and narrative transformation. In an age in which technology affords writers and other producers and mediators of text opportunities to work across modes and media, it is perhaps scarcely surprising that the multimodal potential of various forms of storytelling is coming to the fore and that some writers are experimenting with text design and multiple modes of narrative realization. As has been shown, it is in the process of interaction of the various modes and media employed that new ways of configuring aspects of experience (real or imagined) are brought into circulation and made visible.

The present chapter will also be concerned with notions of translation in relation to modes of representation but will focus on language and culture as resources which can be deployed, both critically and creatively, to produce new narratives. While the two novels chosen as case studies, Monica Ali's *Brick Lane* (2004) and Xiaolu Guo's *A Concise Chinese-English Dictionary for Lovers* (2007) are both written in English, as will be seen, they represent main protagonists experiencing a situation in which cultural differences are foregrounded and where questions of language and voice are thematized. More specifically, they deal with issues of translation both metaphorically and literally.

In *Brick Lane* this manifests itself in terms of the experiences, filtered through a third-person narrator, of a young Bangladeshi woman, Nazneen, who has come to England for an arranged marriage and from whose perspective the reader encounters cultural differences between life in Gouripur, Bangladesh and Tower Hamlets, London. In addition, the intercalation into the narrative of the story of Nazneen's sister, Hasina, relayed through a series of letters in 'pidgin' English, raises questions not only about the translation of experience and cultural representations in a broad sense but also potentially about translation in a narrower sense.

This comparative, cultural perspective is complicated by the fact that Nazneen arrives in England alone, with no English, and must learn to accommodate to her new situation. With time and distance, this situation changes: Nazneen begins to work from home, has an affair and eventually exerts a measure of independence. Unlike her husband, Chanu, whose prospects in England do not chime with his ambitions and who eventually returns to Bangladesh, Nazneen comes to find a place for herself and her two daughters in East London. Her initial homesickness and fond childhood memories are replaced by a stronger sense of self-worth and an increasing ability to control her circumstances.

Likewise, *A Concise Chinese-English Dictionary for Lovers* (hereafter *Dictionary for Lovers*) tells the story of a young Chinese woman's encounter with life in London over a one-year period, in the course of which she acquires a boyfriend and an increasingly sophisticated English syntax and vocabulary. Aspects of both Chinese and English culture are filtered through her narrative consciousness in often humorous and sometimes poignant prose presented in the form of extensive dictionary entries which highlight cultural, as well as lexical, differences. While within the storyworld, the main character, Z, is trying to make sense of English culture for herself (relative to the culture and language from which she has come), she is also effectively 'translating' Chinese culture for an Anglophone audience, while drawing attention to the ways in which linguistic routines and habits can reflect deep-seated cultural preferences and prejudices.

Furthermore, at a point in the story when Z is tired of struggling to express herself through another language, she resorts to writing a dictionary entry in Chinese with a supposed editor's translation into English. It is significant that the entry comes under 'nonsense', whose meaning is defined as 'something that has or makes no sense; absurd language; foolish behaviour' (Guo, 2007, p. 179), a gloss which reflects Z's feelings at that moment about the futility of trying to communicate in English.

With the rise of English as a global language or lingua franca, seemingly at the expense of other major world languages, it is all the more important to recognize the potential of language and culture as a narrative resource. In the two case studies that follow, I wish to emphasize the role of cultural translation in these works and indicate how access to or knowledge of other languages and cultures is not simply a precondition for deployment of a particular thematic but also creates the necessary conditions for innovation in language use and the production of new generic forms. Unlike Trivedi (2007), for whom expansion of the concept of translation risks leading to 'a wholly translated, monolingual, monocultural, monolithic world' (p. 286), I shall argue that writing in English, far from being monolithic, bears traces of its multiple origins and that writers who are products of more than one language and culture are best placed to create works of fiction that draw on a range of narrative resources. From this perspective, the specificity of different languages and cultures is not undermined and lost but reworked in a materially different setting, giving rise to new literary and linguistic possibilities. What can result are texts that call attention to the richness and diversity of their 'translated' material and cultural base/s and open up a multidimensional reading space which requires readers to engage with difference and 'otherness'.

This notion of the multidimensional text draws on Hicks's (1991) work on border writing, in which she examines the consequences for narrative (from both a writer's and reader's perspective) of particular types of 'border' location, in both a literal and a metaphoric sense. While she is primarily concerned with the work of Latin American writers with access to both English and Spanish and/or consciousness of the mix of cultures informing their social and literary histories, some of the points she makes have relevance beyond the borders of North and South America. One of the characteristics of border writing which she examines, a preference for a 'strategy of translation rather than representation', whereby 'border writers ultimately undermine the distinction between original and alien culture' (Hicks, 1991, p. xxiii) is consistent with a view that experience of difference goes beyond the articulation of binary oppositions. Of particular interest in the present context is Hicks's contention that border writers tend to emphasize 'the multiplicity of languages within any single language' (p. xxiii), a position reflecting the sensitivity of writers who are the product of more than one language and/or culture to the creative and critical possibilities inherent in language itself.

Translating Culture and Cultural Translation

Trivedi's (2007) review of the parallel and overlapping development of Translation Studies and Postcolonial Studies is reflected in what he sets out as an opposition between 'translating culture' and 'cultural translation'. The first expression is used by Trivedi to refer to the process of translating works originally written in another language as a means of extending knowledge of a source culture to a target culture or cultures. The second is taken to relate to usage in postcolonial and post-structuralist discourses to refer to a much broader view of translation, whereby migrant subjects are translated from one culture to another. In the context of a focus on migration and multiculturalism, Trivedi (2007) is wary of the ways in which the material specificity of particular languages and cultures is glossed over in favour of a more abstract concern with human migrancy, its processes and conditions.

Reviewing trends in Translation Studies, Trivedi (2007) traces a move from a primarily linguistic approach to translation where the task of the translator is seen as substituting one set of linguistic signs for another in a different language to greater interest in language as a carrier of culture-specific items and of the translation of literary texts, in particular, as requiring 'a more complex negotiation between two cultures' (Trivedi, 2007, p. 280) than that implied by the notion of linguistic transfer. 'Increasingly now', he continues, 'comparative studies of literature across languages have become the concern of Translation Studies; it is the translational tail that now wags the comparative dog' (p. 281). At the same time as he notes a cultural turn in Translation Studies, he points to a nascent interest in Cultural Studies in translation, notwithstanding the fact that the language of its key texts is English, and a turn in Postcolonial Studies towards cultural translation, a term which originated in social anthropology (cf. Asad, 1986) and was picked up by postcolonial theorists such as Bhabha (1994).

Asad's (1986) critique of the implicitly Western values permeating the discourses and modes of thought of social anthropologists from first-world countries as they represent and translate the social, cultural and religious practices and behaviours of largely third-world peoples revolves around the consequences of inequality in the languages used. The tribesman whose cultural practices have been represented and interpreted by the Western social anthropologist is, by and large, not in a position to contest that representation. The power to create and authorize meaning/s about the other culture lies, therefore, with the writer as translator of that culture. Even as he attempts to situate cultural difference sympathetically in relation to the specific contexts in which it is inscribed, in rendering another culture into a language familiar to his academic peers and members of the target culture, the social anthropologist is abstracting away from his experience of the source culture and representing it relative to his own culture's preferred discourses and modes of thought.

This basic power differential in the representation of other cultures is one of the strands which Robinson (1997) identifies in postcolonial approaches to translation. He examines the role of translation in the creation and maintenance of empire and looks at the strategies adopted by postcolonial writers for resisting or challenging the imposition of a dominant set of cultural representations. One of the strategies he points to is that of hybridization and linguistic creolization. Having grown up in societies where a language was imposed on the colonized by the colonizers, usually in the domains of education and administration (e.g. French in North Africa), rather than conform to a strict separation of those languages for different purposes (e.g. French at school, Arabic in religious contexts and a local dialect to communicate with family and friends), some postcolonial writers are mixing their languages or inflecting one with the accents of the other (cf. Robinson, 1997, pp. 100–3). In these circumstances, notions of translation into and out of a single language are complicated, as is the notion of the superiority of one language over another.

For Bhabha (1994, p. 319), the 'borderline negotiations of cultural translation' serve to open up spaces for 'reinscription or redescription' (p. 324). He posits a third space where 'difference is neither One nor the Other but *something else besides, in-between*' (p. 313; italics in original). In looking at the work of Rushdie, Bhabha (1994) focuses on the 'indeterminacy of diasporic

identity' (322) and points to 'the performativity of translation as the staging of
cultural difference' (325). In examining the furore over Rushdie's *The Satanic
Verses* (1988), Bhabha (1994, p. 322) points to 'the anxiety of the irresolvable,
borderline culture of hybridity' and sees this as a factor in the strong reactions
to Rushdie's book, since, from a fundamentalist perspective: 'Hybridity is
heresy' (Bhabha, 1994, p. 322). He reads Rushdie's blasphemy in relation to
'the staging of cross-genre, cross-cultural identities' (p. 323). What Bhabha sees
as 'a poetics of relocation and reinscription' (p. 323) can be viewed as explosive
from the perspective of a belief in the 'purity of origins' (p. 323). Likewise, in
relation to a poem by Walcott on the colonization of the Caribbean, Bhabha
(1994) shows how 'the postcolonial, migrant community in-difference' (p. 335)
is constituted by and emerges from an inscription of opposing versions of
history.

The potentials of this situation, whereby writers have access to other versions of history and different languages which inevitably carry traces of their
different cultural formations, are highlighted in Maier (1995), for whom the
bilingual or multilingual individual has come to embody the practice of what
she calls cross-cultural translation. For Maier (1995), notions of loss and gain
which are often evoked in relation to the bilingual condition – we might
think here of works such as Eva Hoffman's (1998) *Lost in Translation* or Ariel
Dorfman's (1999) *Heading South, Looking North: A Bilingual Journey* – are but
one set of discourses surrounding discussion of life in two languages and
processes of translation. Others are emerging which reflect the new realities
of life for people living, for example, on the border between countries (e.g.
Mexico and the US) or enjoying a mixed cultural heritage (cf. the new mestiza
consciousness of writers such as Gloria Anzaldúa cited in Robinson, 1997,
p. 103). These discourses do not privilege one language and culture at the
expense of the other but permit their co-existence not necessarily in a seamless
blend but in a spirit of *intimacy* and mutual *inquiry* (the terms in italics are
Maier's 1995, pp. 28–33). Thus many writers today are working across and
between languages and cultures and are, in effect, engaging in an ongoing
process of translation.

Writing as an Intercultural Process: The Space 'Between'

In situating writing as an intercultural process, Malcolm (1999) focuses on the
situation of Australian Aboriginals in the context of bilingual education programmes. He points to the sometimes conflicting agendas of the indigenous
people keen to hold on to their languages and cultural traditions and that of
educational institutions intent on providing access to the linguistic and cultural
mainstream. While Malcolm's context is apparently far removed from a concern with highly educated and literate writers of fiction, some of his more
general points have a bearing on the present discussion, since he talks about

the effects of the adoption of particular kinds of socially sanctioned literacy practices on individuals and discusses their possible consequences for cultural identity. Insofar as the present context relates to writers with experience of other languages and cultures, whose works treat issues of cultural identity and thematize the relationship between language and representation, the notion of writing as intercultural process is clearly relevant.

Although not explicitly defined, the context of Malcolm's discussion situates writing as an intercultural process in relation to an accommodation between different systems, whether these systems relate to different modes of writing (spoken vs. written, for example) within a culture or to differing conventions across languages and cultures. He recognizes that while for some individuals or groups such an accommodation can be construed positively in terms of providing an alternative means of representation or an addition to the communicative repertoire, for others the intercultural is less a space which allows different cultures to be bridged and more a gap between usually unequal and often incommensurable modes of representation.

In relation to translation from a postcolonial perspective, Robinson (1997) points to interest in power relations between countries and how this might affect processes of translation. In representing other cultures, it is therefore important to be aware of the historical and political relations that have existed between and among countries and to situate translation and the role of the translator not as a neutral process but in the light of social, cultural and economic realities. He is referring here not just to translation in the narrow sense of linguistic transfer from a source text (ST) to a target text (TT) but in a wider sense which embraces all forms of cultural representation. For in representing a culture, be it one's own or that of another, the writer 'translates' his/her vision into words which necessarily mediate and evaluate what they seek to represent. In this sense all writing is a kind of translation; however, where there is a power differential between nations and languages, the question of representation can become vexed. From this perspective, the issue of who is authorized to represent or give voice to a culture and that of the language used becomes a highly political one (cf. reactions to *Brick Lane*). This situation is further complicated in contemporary society by two phenomena: migration and multiculturalism, as a result of which there can be no assumption of a one-to-one correspondence between nation state and language or nation state and ethnicity.

In the case of Monica Ali, who is herself the product of two cultures as the daughter of an English mother and a Bangladeshi father, with whom she moved from Bangladesh to England at a young age, there is clearly an interest in the experience of those who migrate. This interest is apparent not only in *Brick Lane* but, in different ways, in subsequent novels. Whether it be the lives of incomers to a small village in southern Portugal and their impact on the locals as in *Alentejo Blue* (2006) or the dependence of a large London hotel on migrant workers in *In the Kitchen* (2009), Ali's novelistic terrain appears to revolve around the outsider or those living on the margins of society in one way or another either through choice, or more often than not, necessity.

Interest in the acquisition of a new language and culture is very obviously foregrounded in Guo's *Dictionary for Lovers* (2007), given the novel's use of a deliberately broken but progressively improving English. Like her protagonist Z, Guo also made the journey from East to West, arriving in London in 2002 on a film scholarship. While her own experience of life in London cannot be assumed to coincide with that of her main protagonist Z in *Dictionary for Lovers* (2007), there are some parallels which may be seen to inform the narrative. Guo has lived in Hackney where the novel is set and kept a diary of her experiences and observations. In the novel Z takes her dictionary and notebook everywhere so that she can check meanings and write down new words, in the hope that by expanding her vocabulary, she can increase her ability to come to terms with her new reality.

As Guo explains in an interview with Sheena Patel (25 March 2009), the structure of her novel in terms of the dictionary entries and the use of broken English were the first things to come to her.

> I thought I would like to write a novel based on broken English or foreign English. That foreign English had to be the character of the whole book. In order to create that style I had to somehow mock a kind of dictionary – like the Oxford dictionary to establish a kind of characteristic type structure and then when the character speaks in broken English then, I think, the whole novel gains a meaning from the broken down vocabulary, like a dictionary.

This very conscious attempt to reflect the protagonist's increasing grasp of the syntax and lexis of English as she negotiates cultural and linguistic difficulties is indicative of Guo's interest in language (and indeed genre) as resource.

Focusing on each of the novels in turn, the remainder of the chapter will examine *Brick Lane* and *Dictionary for Lovers* with a view to demonstrating their use of translation as a mode in developing a particular thematics as well as in relation to questions of the construction of narrative voice and perspective. I shall begin by setting the works in question in the broader context of Ali's and Guo's other works.

Monica Ali's *Brick Lane*

While in many ways a publishing and critical success, *Brick Lane* (2003) also provoked a measure of controversy among the Bangladeshi community in Brick Lane, a controversy which reignited following the decision to adapt the novel into a film, released in 2007, by Sarah Gavron. What appeared to be at the heart of the problem was the perception of Ali's portrayal of Bangladeshis as 'uneducated and unsophisticated' (Cacciottolo, 2006) and an assumption of identification between Ali's fictional representation of a part of East London and the realities of the lives of its real Bangladeshi inhabitants. While the protests over *Brick Lane* cannot be compared to the vehemence of those in connection with Rushdie's *Satanic Verses*, the fact that it elicited vocal criticism is evidence of the potential dangers of attempting to represent cultural difference and to act as a kind of cultural mediator or translator.

Within the context of a focus on cultural translation and discussions of the intercultural narrative, there are a number of issues to be addressed. These relate to what Cormack (2006) characterizes as the politics of narrative form and the relationship between migrant content and forms of realism. Cormack's (2006, p. 696) contention is that 'to depict Britain's new hybrid society through realism is not the same as to depict it through other representational modes'. He goes on to argue that narrative voice and focalization conspire to construct the subjectivity of the main character, Nazneen, in particular ways. Specifically, he sees her as a character whose growth is dependent on putting aside aspects of her earlier enculturation (e.g. a belief in and acceptance of fate) and assuming a greater sense of personal agency. Insofar as such a trajectory is common to the Western Bildungsroman or novel of education, Cormack (2006) sees Nazneen as conforming to a model of personal growth and development privileged in the realist novel.

In addition, he points to the issue of translation in the novel and its various uses of English. For Cormack (2006, p. 710), 'English does not appear to be remade but rather is used intact, as a novelistic lingua franca, and it is this that generates the effect of realism.' These remarks relate to the previous point about narrative voice and focalization in the sense that the reader sees the world through Nazneen's eyes but her experience is conveyed by a third-person narrator who speaks the kind of English we cannot assume Nazneen to know, particularly on her arrival in Britain. Moreover, while Cormack (2006) acknowledges ambivalence in the fact that Hasina's letters are reproduced, seemingly unmediated, in 'pidgin' English, he concludes that the 'surface of realism' is 'stretched' but not broken (p. 716). Ultimately, he reads *Brick Lane* as a novel which argues that: 'One may overcome the problems of postcolonial identity [. . .] through transcending history and achieving self-authorship' (p. 717). It is, therefore, according to Cormack (2006), a less radical work than Rushdie's *The Satanic Verses*. However, he concedes that unlike the realist novels of the nineteenth century, *Brick Lane* makes visible 'the relationship between form and content [. . .]: we see them at work, when we are usually asked to take them for granted' (p. 719).

Cormack's points are related in the sense that narrative voice – who speaks? – has a bearing on what the reader perceives to be the case, albeit through the eyes of a particular character – who sees? – as well as on mode of evaluation in terms of narrative discourse. In the course of the novel there are degrees of mediation or narrative intervention at work which relate, among other things, to choice of scene or summary, that is to say the extent to which dialogue is used rather than a summary of events reported by the narrator. In addition, the fact that events and perceptions are focalized through Nazneen means that even though she is not telling her own story in her own words (cf. first-person narrative), there are moments when the distance between narrator and protagonist is minimized and the reader has the illusion of being inside Nazneen's mind.

The extent to which different narrative techniques are employed sometimes even within the same paragraph so that the reader moves from an external to an internal view and from reported speech to free indirect speech can be seen in the example below. The passage on which I shall focus comes early on in the book (Ali, 2004, p. 18) and is situated in the context of a larger extract (pp. 17–21) relating the events in a day in Nazneen's life six months after arriving in England. She is shown to have developed a household routine and appears to have settled in. However, her nostalgia for what she has left behind and her bouts of loneliness are reflected in the comparisons made between her current life in Tower Hamlets, 1985 and her recollection of childhood in Gouripur, in what had been East Pakistan.

At the beginning of the extract, from which the passage for analysis is taken, Nazneen is shown to be waving at one of her neighbours from across the way, someone to whom she has never spoken but whose person and movements she has observed from her window. Her fascination with the tattoo lady, who seems to be quite unlike other women she has met, is evident in the descriptions which emphasize Nazneen's role as observer of a foreign culture, taking note of the behaviours and actions of one of its members from within the confines of her flat. That Nazneen finds the environment somewhat alien is reflected in the descriptions and evaluations of what she is reported to see (e.g. 'the dead grass and broken paving stones' (p. 17); 'the stiff English capitals' (p. 18) on a sign in English, with 'the curlicues beneath' (p. 18) in Bengali, prohibiting dumping, parking and ball games). The block of flats is portrayed as joyless and drab, a place where dogs defecate and the air is 'thick with the smell from the over-flowing communal bins' (p. 18).

In comparison with her rather drab surroundings, the tattoo lady cuts a colourful figure with two-thirds of visible flesh covered in ink. Despite the fact that Chanu has told Nazneen that their neighbour is a Hell's Angel, Nazneen is still drawn to her and imagines her tattoos to be flowers or birds. It is as if, despite their obvious differences, the two women have something in common, their status as outsiders, perhaps, or their shared sense of isolation. It is interesting that Nazneen sees in the tattoo lady's 'look of boredom and detachment' (Ali, 2004, p. 18) a reflection of the kind of state sought by the sadhus or holy men as they walk in rags through the villages, seeming not to notice their surroundings or care about their material well-being. In this way, the unfamiliar is translated into more familiar terms and cultural points of reference from Nazneen's former existence are brought to bear on aspects of her new life.

This is the context in which Nazneen's thoughts are presented, as reproduced below (Ali, 2004, p. 18).

[1] Six months now since she'd been sent away to London. [2] Every morning before she opened her eyes she thought, *if I were the wishing type, I know what I would wish.* [3] And then she opened her eyes and saw Chanu's puffy face on the pillow next to her, his lips parted indignantly even as he slept. [4] She saw the pink dressing table with the curly-sided mirror, and the monstrous black wardrobe that claimed most of the room. [5] Was it cheating? [6] To think, *I know what I would wish?* [7] Was it not the same as making the wish? [8] If she knew what the wish would be, then somewhere in her heart she had already made it. (Italics in original but sentence numbers added for ease of reference)

The above passage illustrates Ali's narrative technique in terms of a move from reporting what Nazneen sees and does to inhabiting her thoughts. In the wake of the final sentence of the previous paragraph: 'The breeze on Nazneen's face was thick with the smell from the over-flowing communal bins' (Ali, 2004, p. 18), sentence 1 appears to be a simple narratorial report of the length of time that has now passed since Nazneen's arrival. However, the omission of the expected [It was] from the sentence gives it a more colloquial feel, introducing the possibility of Nazneen (rather than the authorial narrator) reviewing in her mind the length of her stay. This reading appears plausible given the fact that sentence 2 introduces a directly reported thought attributed to Nazneen. Indeed the italicized '*if I were the wishing type, I know what I would wish*' is a graphic marker of the fact that there has been a shift from indirect to direct speech and from third person to first person. However the introductory tag, 'she thought' is a reminder of the narratorial presence. It is as if within the reporting structure of what Nazneen is represented as doing every day – emerging from sleep, opening her eyes and looking around her – the reader moves from looking *at* Nazneen to looking *with* her and switches from an external to an internal viewpoint.

This feeling of inhabiting Nazneen's consciousness and even of hearing her express her thoughts is strengthened by the fact that the reporting tag or framing clause is subsequently dropped. Sentences 5–7 appear to come from Nazneen as she reflects on what she has been wishing for just before she opens her eyes. Yet the final sentence of the paragraph, sentence 8, makes clear by grammatical means – If she knew – that these are free indirect thoughts. As Toolan (2001: 135), indicates, using free indirect speech or free indirect thought is 'a strategy of (usually temporary or discontinuous) alignment, in words, values and perspective, of the narrator with a character'. It is, therefore, a narrative means for permitting access within a third-person narrative to the consciousness of a protagonist and reducing the degree of visible mediation on the part of the narrator. As Cormack (2006) points out, at a time when Nazneen 'could say two things in English: sorry and thank you' (Ali, 2004, p. 19), this identification and articulation of her thoughts in English is ultimately attributable to the authorial narrator, who has, in effect, inscribed and trans-lated Nazneen's thoughts, which by definition are unspoken and inaccessible, from Bengali into English.

Another aspect of the narrative technique employed by Ali (2004) to situate her character relates to the manner in which description not only functions to set the scene and provide a sense of the kind of environment in which Nazneen finds herself but also serves to evaluate Nazneen's perceptions of that environment. I have already referred to the description of what Nazneen sees as she looks out of the window towards 'the dead grass and broken paving stones' (Ali, 2004, p. 17), epithets which give an indication of the rather depressing state of the surrounding area. By contrast, when later that afternoon Nazneen drifts off to sleep on the sofa, what she sees in her mind's eye is described in rather more lyrical terms.

> She looked out across jade-green rice fields and swam in the cool dark lake. She walked arm-in-arm to school with Hasina, and skipped part of the way [. . .]. And heaven, which was above, was wide and empty and the land stretched out ahead and she could see to the very end of it, where the earth smudged the sky in a dark blue line. (Ali, 2004, p. 21)

Compared to the enclosed, claustrophobic feel of her new environment in Tower Hamlets, Nazneen's dreamy recollection of her girlhood home is described in terms which emphasize the expansive and lush nature of the environment and express a sense of freedom and lack of restriction. It is the terms of the comparison which leave the reader in no doubt that Nazneen's current situation in a flat stuffed with furniture, including the presence in the bedroom of a '*monstrous* black wardrobe' (Ali, 2004, p. 18; the italics are mine), is not one which strikes an imaginative chord. Her response to her environment and the fact that she is constantly having to check her behaviour (e.g. 'She should be getting on with the evening meal' (Ali, 2004, p. 19)) and remind herself of her good fortune in having married well (p. 21) is indicative of a degree of dissatisfaction with her lot and prepares the reader for what will happen later in the novel – her affair with Karim.

The trajectory which Nazneen follows can be seen to be motivated right from the start of the novel. Whether this is viewed in terms of personal growth and development or in relation to an accommodation to her environment is debatable. Certainly, the fact that Nazneen ends the affair with Karim and decides to remain in East London with Shahana and Bibi, while Chanu goes on alone to Bangladesh, can be interpreted as Nazneen taking control of her life rather than simply submitting to fate or to the will of others. The book ends with Nazneen being taken by her two daughters and her friend and business partner, Razia, to an ice-skating rink, a scene which recalls a much earlier one in the novel where Nazneen is captivated by the ice-skating on television. Her unfamiliarity with this strange yet beautiful practice is reflected in the manner in which her observations are 'translated' through the discourse (p. 36). The sentence structure and choice of lexis are used to represent ice-skating from the perspective of someone who has never seen it before and who is trying to make sense of it. In this respect, ice-skating operates at a number of levels in the novel simultaneously: it represents an unfamiliar cultural practice requiring interpretation; in its tightly choreographed movements and close interactions between a pair of dancers, one male, one female, it prefigures Nazneen's romantic entanglement with Karim; and it opens up spaces of possibility, including the possibility of self-definition.

The various ways in which the concept of translation operates in the novel requires further elaboration. First, there is a representation of aspects of British culture as it is perceived and experienced by the main characters, Nazneen and her family. The reader also gets a sense of the extent to which some of the other characters such as Razia, Karim, and Dr Azad and his wife experience life in Britain. Second, Bangladesh is represented indirectly and in comparison with Britain through Nazneen's recollections of her girlhood and in relation to Chanu's insistence that his daughters, Shahana and Bibi, learn something of their 'originary' culture, despite having been born in Britain. But it is through Hasina's letters that the reader, arguably, has more direct contact with aspects of life in Bangladesh, as she describes her rather picaresque and somewhat difficult existence.

In many ways, Hasina serves to set up a kind of opposition in the novel between different paths taken in life. While Nazneen has accepted her fate, at least to begin with, and agreed to an arranged marriage, Hasina marries for love. When her marriage fails, she moves to Dhaka and becomes a machinist but gradually finds herself taken advantage of by the man she believed to be like a father to her. Moving from one unsatisfactory situation to the next, she eventually finds work looking after the children of a well-to-do family, before finally running off with the cook. The realities of Hasina's material struggle, rendered through her letters, and her depiction of the situation of women in Bangladesh contrast with the relative stability of Nazneen's domestic situation. While life in Britain also has its dramas – Chanu gets into debt and is at the mercy of the moneylender, Mrs Islam – Hasina's letters are a reminder of the tougher economic and social realities in Bangladesh.

The question of why Hasina's letters are written in a form of English which marks them as 'foreign' is one which merits discussion, the more so since they appear in the context of a novel featuring a central protagonist who comes to England with very little English and whose thoughts are nevertheless rendered in native-speaker-like English. As will be seen in relation to Guo's (2007) *Dictionary for Lovers*, the use of pidgin or broken English can be a conscious narrative strategy linked to the themes of the story. In relation to *Brick Lane*, I wish to suggest that the *form*, including the 'faulty' syntax of

Hasina's letters can be read as a kind of foreignization (cf. Venuti, 1993). By foreignization, I mean to refer to a translation strategy which, far from striving to erase (cultural and linguistic) difference in order to produce a text in translation which reads as if it were originally written in the target language, seeks a mode of expression which draws attention to linguistic and cultural difference.

However, such a view begs the question of whether to read Hasina's letters as if they are in English translation, having been originally written in another language, presumably Bengali, or whether to see them simply as texts designed to mark cultural and social difference, within the context of a novel representing the migrant experience, regardless of their 'originary' language. The issue of the difference in mode of representation of Nazneen's and Hasina's experiences is left unresolved by such an explanation, unless account is also taken of their differing geographic and ultimately economic and social locations. As characters who have taken different paths and whose lives have different dynamics, Nazneen is shown to have come to Britain from Bangladesh for an arranged marriage, while Hasina has left her village in Bangladesh to follow her heart but remains in her country of origin. In this sense, their trajectories can be seen to encode novelistically their different subject positions and degrees of agency.

For Cormack (2006, p. 710), in the case of Nazneen, '[t]ranslation as productive impossibility has been replaced by an unproblematic rendering of one culture's signifying systems in another's'. By this, he means to point to the fact that with few exceptions (e.g. Chanu's correction of Nazneen's pronunciation of 'ice-skating', (Ali, 2004, pp. 36–7)), the novel progresses as if Nazneen were a speaker of English and fails to problematize its representation, through the medium of English, of her experience. The reader learns that Nazneen's request to learn English has been turned down by husband Chanu, who feels that there is no need (p. 37). Yet it appears over time that Nazneen manages to learn some English from television, radio and from her limited social interactions.

Clearly, there are practical constraints and questions of audience at issue here. As a British writer of fiction, albeit from a mixed cultural and ethnic background, Ali is clearly unlikely to write in anything other than English. Furthermore, she appears to be writing about issues of class and ethnicity as well as of the effects of cultural difference for an international, English-speaking audience. Nevertheless, Cormack's concern with the implications of linguistic choice and the consequences of a particular mode of representation are not without merit. It is perhaps in this context that Hasina's letters can be seen as providing a counter-narrative to the main narrative in that in their manner of articulation, they refuse to be domesticated, just as Hasina herself finally prefers a life of adventure and of mobility to one of stasis and domesticity. While Nazneen eschews the possibility of a move back to Bangladesh with Chanu, preferring to remain in East London with her daughters, Hasina ends up on the road.

Xiaolu Guo's *A Concise Chinese-English Dictionary for Lovers*

As a writer, rather than a film-maker, Xiaolu Guo first came to prominence in the UK with the publication in 2007 of *Dictionary for Lovers*. Shortlisted for the Orange Prize for Fiction, Guo's work came to the attention of a wider public in the same year in which she had been longlisted for the newly established Man Booker Asian Prize for *20 Fragments of a Ravenous Youth* (hereafter *Fragments*), a book which would see publication in the UK in 2008. Since then, Guo's output, both cinematographic and literary, has been prolific. In addition to *Dictionary for Lovers* (2007) and *Fragments* (2008), she has published a further novel, *UFO in Her Eyes* (2009) and a collection of short stories, *Lovers in the Age of Indifference* (2010). In the same period, she has produced a number of films, both documentary and feature, the most recent of which are *She, A Chinese* (2009) and *Once Upon a Time Proletarian* (2009).

Guo's dual background as a writer and a film-maker is germane to the present chapter in a number of ways. For alongside Guo's concern with language and the extent to which a writer is able to manipulate it in order to express his/her vision and communicate with others, is an interest in the complementary power of the image. Within her fiction, Guo explores the potential of the novelistic form to incorporate aspects of the visual. While this tendency is already evident to some extent in *Dictionary for Lovers* (2007), it is more pronounced in *UFO in Her Eyes* (2009). For example, in *Dictionary for Lovers* the story of Z's arrival in Heathlow (sic) airport is accompanied by two visual representations ostensibly taken from her passport (Guo, 2007, p. 4), as she goes through immigration, and later as she reads through her lover's private diaries and letters, there are reproductions of handwritten extracts complete with crossed-out words (pp. 90–9).

Guo's decision to tell Z's story via a series of dictionary entries can also be seen to result in a further visual dimension, since, at the top of the page on the left-hand side, in place of chapter headings, there are terms, such as 'alien', 'privacy' 'drifter', presented in large font and emboldened. These terms are then repeated in smaller font and are followed by their dictionary meanings. The subsequent narrative and commentary resumes after a space left to separate the entry from a recounting of an episode or episodes in the ongoing narrative illustrative of points of difficulty or difference, which have emerged between the two main characters and/or their representative cultures.

UFO in Her Eyes (2009) takes this strategy much further insofar as the story progresses by means of a series of case files compiled by the state and local police responsible for investigating the alleged sighting of a UFO by a peasant woman. Extracts from numbered documents and the transcripts of interviews are reproduced. The very paperclips used to group papers together are represented visually to afford an illusion of 'authenticity'. In other words, visual culture and the affordances of the visual are imported into what might reasonably be assumed to be a predominantly verbal medium.

At the same time, Guo's interest in what it might mean for an individual to cross cultures, to inhabit a different space and to come to terms with a different reality are all themes which she explores in both her films and her novels, though clearly the different media make different demands in relation to how the story is told and the narrative is progressed. Concern with travel and migration against the backdrop of globalization and a fast changing world is a theme which is picked up both novelistically and cinematographically. Not only can the novel *UFO in Her Eyes* (2009) be read as a critique of the impact of capitalism and entrepreneurialism on the lives of peasants in rural China but *She, A Chinese* (2009), the film, deals with various forms of exploitation, in both the private and public domains, as the main character seizes the opportunity to leave China and move to London on the violent death of her boyfriend.

It is in *Dictionary for Lovers* (2007), however, that the focus on language and culture and the embeddedness of language in culture is most extensively treated. The novel is essentially the story of a love affair between two people from different cultures over the space of a year. Z arrives in London to learn English and finds herself moving in with an Englishman 20 years her senior after meeting him at the cinema. It is on the basis of a misunderstanding that she moves into his house in Hackney. Having indicated that she would like to see where he lives, he replies 'Be my guest' (Guo, 2007, p. 53), an expression which Z takes literally: 'When you say "guest" I think you meaning I can stay in your house. A week later, I move out from my Chinese landlord' (p. 54).

To begin with, the affair goes well. Z's desire to learn English and increase her vocabulary sits easily with her lover's role as teacher and cultural explicator as well as initiator into a new world of sexual and emotional experience. However, over time cultural and individual differences come between the lovers and a kind of role reversal takes place. As Z becomes more confident in self-expression and voicing her opinions in English, her lover becomes more remote and has less to say for himself. The critical point comes when he decides to visit a friend in the south-west without Z and in his absence she rifles through his diaries and private letters to make a discovery: that he is bisexual and spent a large part of his early adulthood with men.

Shortly after her lover's return, Z reveals the fact that she has read his diaries and letters and they argue about privacy, a concept which appears to differentiate them along broadly cultural lines. For Z, as a young Chinese woman, the idea of keeping secrets from her lover is anathema and reflects a difference in culture:

But why people need privacy? Why privacy is important? In China, every family live together, grandparents, parents, daughter, son, and their relatives too. Eat together and share everything, talk about everything. Privacy makes people lonely. Privacy make people fall apart. (Guo, 2007, p. 106)

As their argument continues, Z characterizes him as a drifter and another difference emerges in respect of their concepts of time and the ability to plan for the future. For her lover:

the future is about moving on, to some new place. I don't know where I am going. It's like I am riding a horse through the desert, and the horse just carries me somewhere, maybe with an oasis, but I don't know. (Guo, 2007, p. 107)

For Z family and belonging is important, as is having a clear sense of direction, whereas for her lover, 'It's important to be able to live with uncertainty' (Guo, 2007, p. 108).

Significantly, the next dictionary entry on intimacy begins with a question: 'How can *intimate* live with *privacy*?' (Guo, 2007, p. 109; italics in original). In this entry Z reflects on their different aspirations and desires. She situates her lover's desire to maintain his sense of self and his independence in the context of a society where '[p]eople keep distance' (p. 109) and even lovers don't always live together but 'see each other at weekend or sleep together twice a week' (p. 109). She sees Westerners as being 'more separated, lonely' (p. 109) than Chinese people where 'family means everything' (p. 109). Yet this is also the entry where Z recounts her lover taking her to see a wood full of beech trees, clearly a place of significance to him. In the 'dark, lush, and wet' (p. 110) woods, they make love and seal the bond between them.

However, this is also an episode which reveals linguistic differences. To begin with Z understands her lover to be taking them to a place called Burnham Beach, since she knows he loves the sea and she is keen to visit the ocean. However, she soon discovers that he is using the homophone 'beech' to refer to a type of tree. This misunderstanding gives rise to a reflection on the difficulties of English compared to Chinese. In Chinese, Z thinks, the same word can have different meanings but at least these are signalled by the tone, whereas in English there is no change in tone and she wonders how she will ever come to understand such a complicated language. While at one level the misunderstanding is intended to be humorous, it also points to an aspect of English which can make learning the language difficult: in spoken language, it is impossible to tell the difference between 'beach' and 'beech' unless the context is such as to clearly differentiate the meanings.

This consciousness of the rootedness of communication practices in the features of the particular language used to communicate and its relationship to the culture in which it is embedded or to which it refers is one of the key features of *Dictionary for Lovers*. As a native Chinese-speaker and learner of English, Z comes up against and uncovers aspects of the English language which jar with features of Chinese and which seem to reveal deeper levels of understanding about the respective cultures. For example, early on in the narrative, she is overwhelmed by the tenses in English and contrasts them with Chinese which she thinks of as being simpler and over which she can exercise control. In Chinese, there are '[n]o verb-change usage, no tense differences, no gender changes. We bosses of our language. But English language is boss of English user' (Guo, 2007, p. 24). She goes on to point to further differences between English and Chinese which she feels to be significant of deeper, cultural differences, such as the ordering in Chinese of concepts of time and place at the beginning of a sentence to reflect the place of humans in the larger universe, whereas English allows human action and endeavour to come first relegating time and place to a secondary position. In an effort to relate grammatical systems to larger social and cultural issues, Z speculates that the dominant positioning of the subject in English reflects the focus on individualism, whereas in China it would seem immodest to put self first (p. 26).

In a radio interview with Rick Kleffel in 2007, Guo makes clear that language itself is a central character in the novel and that she spent a whole year reworking the first 20 or so pages of the novel so as to create a Chinese kind of English with its own grammatical system. In essence, Guo has created a kind of interlanguage, though from a position of knowledge rather than ignorance, since she went back to the beginning after drafting the novel and at a point where she had much greater understanding of English than her character had had at that point. As Guo indicates in the interview, it was important 'to set up the broken English in a certain way' and to express through the medium of English the sensibility of a naïve, young Chinese woman encountering English language and culture for the first time in a fresh and authentic way.

So Guo focused in the process of composition not just on the storytelling side but also on the linguistic side. She is conscious of having had to infuse her use of English with traces of Chinese and speaks about her decision to use only the present tense at the beginning of the novel, add the -ing form, and employ simple sentences. Later, in line with the character's increasing grasp of English, she is able to employ more complex sentences with subordinate clauses, to use a range of tenses and show understanding of the pronominal system, which allows the speaker to represent herself as both subject and object of a sentence. This ability to manipulate language to demonstrate or reflect various stages of linguistic development is in itself a tour-de-force. Guo's understanding of language, however, goes far beyond syntactic and lexical forms. She demonstrates her character's struggle to adapt to English ways of thinking and behaving and, at the same time, shows her resistance to the perceived imposition of a way of life with which that character feels uncomfortable, as Chinese and English value systems collide.

From this perspective, Guo sees Z's sexual awakening as both individual and cultural insofar as she has to negotiate what Guo refers to as the differences between 'industrialized' and 'natural' sex. In going to a peep-show in Soho in response to a curiosity about issues that had been taboo in China, she finds herself having to adjust her desires to an industrial model of sex. In a society where, according to Guo, pornographic magazines sit on the supermarket shelves alongside bread and croissants and where the media affects the natural you, Z's desires are filtered through cultural channels. Her lover encourages her to be more independent and sends her on a journey round Europe in the course of which she meets several men and has sex with one of them in Portugal. Motivated by loneliness and the absence of her lover, what starts as an inclination to explore and satisfy her own desire sours with the reality of her encounter with the man in Portugal who enters her against her will in 'a rough, almost violent' (Guo, 2007, p. 252) way. Upon her return to England, realizing she is pregnant and uncertain who the father of the baby is, she has an abortion, after which she feels 'the sorrow of emptiness' (p. 272).

Guo makes clear in the interview (Kleffel, 2007) that there is often a price to pay for youth. She sees her character as naïve and having to come to terms with a world which is less stable and innocent than she had imagined. While Guo acknowledges the effect of cultural differences on her characters, Z and her lover, she also sees them as two sides of a single character struggling to reconcile conflicting emotions and desires. So while the story is indeed about differences in culture, it is also about individual differences and the difficulties human beings have in communicating with one another. For a novel based primarily on linguistic modes of communication, it is also very much concerned with the body. Even as their relationship is unravelling and they are communicating verbally less and less, Z indicates that '[t]he only thing I love completely, without any doubt, is your body. I love it. Temperature. Softness. Forgiveness. Maybe I can let you go, but not your body' (Guo, 2007, p. 313).

Her lover is someone for whom the physical, rather than the mental, world is very important. He loves nature, is a gardener, and an artist, making sculptures of naked men which he displays in the garden and which Z finds ugly. After Z returns to China, she learns in a letter from him that he has finally moved to Wales to be close to the sea. Z is pleased that he appears to have found 'great peace and happiness' (p. 354) at last.

For Guo not only is language important in her work but so is landscape (Kleffel, 2007). As a writer, she indicates that for her character comes out of particular landscapes. So in writing *Dictionary for Lovers*, it was important to create the social landscape of London (Hackney Road, Soho) and Wales. It is the landscape or the cityscape that 'gives you the strength, the force, the reason to write a novel' (Kleffel, 2007). While the focal point of *Dictionary for Lovers* is London, the characters do travel to the south-west and to Wales; encouraged by her lover, Z also goes inter-railing. The reader is therefore able to see the effect of different landscapes on the characters.

At the same time, Guo sees herself 'as a novelist who is on the road [. . .] in an interior sense' (Kleffel, 2007), which might be taken to mean that she is also exploring mental and emotional landscapes. She relates this comment to her interest in poetry, which she sees as 'less physical and more interior' (Kleffel, 2007) but acknowledges that as a writer she needs to be soaked in the life of the society and to find a way of transforming her experience into a form. In this sense, *Dictionary for Lovers* is about 'reading a foreign culture' (Kleffel, 2007) at a level beyond her own experience. She sees it as representing the sum total of all the stories collected of the experiences of foreigners in London glued together and invested in a particular character. The work itself, however, should be 'non-comparable', a term which Guo uses to refer to 'the feeling you are not copying from other people' (Kleffel, 2007). The novel should re-create that 'first-degree feeling' (Kleffel, 2007), the sense of excitement, fear, isolation and so on which might be felt by someone arriving in London from China for the first time as she interacts with the new culture in which she finds herself.

In plotting the story in relation to the arrival and departure a year later of the main protagonist who engages in a love affair with an Englishman, Guo creates a story structure with the potential for drama, as the two characters interact and play out their differences. The grafting of the dictionary form onto the otherwise linear narrative provides a vehicle for a discursive intervention into the novel insofar as the dictionary entries might be seen as interrupting the chronological narrative with definitions and terminology rooted in aspects of culture which prove significant in one way or another to the main protagonist. The form provides a means of commentary on cultural difference as well as an opportunity to narrate episodes illustrative of it.

This narrative innovation in terms of available novel forms in English is, however, also potentially a product of culture, given that Guo is not the first Chinese writer to use the dictionary-novel form (cf. Han Shaogong's *A Dictionary of Maqiao*, written in 1996 and published in English translation in 2003). Nevertheless, in writing in English and availing herself of a generic resource not normally considered in relation to the production of a narrative, Guo has managed to progress the novel form. She acknowledges in interview that '[i]t's quite difficult for [an] author to be experimental [. . .] the risk is you're never going to be published' (Kleffel, 2007) but in this case, the inclusion of a strong storytelling narrative was sufficient to ensure the risks with form were seen by publishers to be justified. In that same interview, she indicated her desire to 'keep testing my own capacity and see where it can end' (Kleffel, 2007), underlining her commitment to trying something new, thereby pushing the novel form forward.

Conclusion

As we have seen, an ability to bring newness into the world is facilitated by access to sets of representational resources, whether linguistic, cultural or generic, which permit writers to test their own capacity and use their differing cultural locations to stretch the novelistic forms they choose and/or combine material in innovative and interesting ways. Through a focus on Monica Ali's

Brick Lane and Xiaolu Guo's *Dictionary for Lovers*, it has been possible to demonstrate how language and cultural difference become resources at a writer's disposal. This is true not simply in terms of the availability of certain types of thematic material but also in relation to mode of expression. A focus on notions of translation as they relate to these two novels has also proved productive in helping to point not just to representations of otherness but, more importantly, to the ways in which language can be used to express compliance with or resistance to a particular status quo. Genre, too, has been shown in the case of Guo to be a creative and critical resource which can be employed in new combinations (such as the dictionary-novel). In sum, modes of creativity have been shown to be dependent on, or at least enhanced by, access to a range of languages and cultures.

Chapter 5

Cultural Transformations of Narrative

Introduction

The idea that writers respond to one another's work, transforming ideas and themes and using or adapting particular narrative structures for their own purposes is not a new one, even if, at various times, it has been differently expressed. Hutcheon (2006, p. 2), for example, remarks that for many writers and critics: 'art is derived from other art; stories are born of other stories'. Notions of influence, though contentious, and notoriously difficult to 'pin down' persist in our culture – witness the recent series of poetry events, organized by the Poetry Society, entitled *Under the Influence* in which contemporary poets talked about the shaping effects on their work of a poet from the past.

In academic culture, Influence Studies has long constituted a branch of Comparative Literature, albeit one subject to contestation and revision in the wake of challenges from literary theory and notions of intertextuality. However, as Guillén's (1993) account of the focus and interests of comparatists show, there remains interest in literary relations and questions of sources, influences and cultural and textual intermediaries, all of which may be seen to affect the production and reception of literature both within and across national boundaries. While such interest may be expressed at the level of documentary evidence (e.g. lists of what writers have read, commented on in diaries, letters and/or notebooks or acknowledged to be 'influential' in their work, including literature in translation), it may also be reflected at the level of thematic and structural parallels and the use of particular leitmotivs in a given work which recall or echo that of another writer or artist.

In this latter sense, there is overlap with other important branches of Comparative Literature as a discipline: thematology, or the study of themes and genology or the study of genres (Guillén, 1993). All of these areas will feature in the present chapter in relation to what I am calling the cultural transformation of narrative. In using this term, I wish to emphasize not only the fact that works of literature, like other cultural artefacts, have histories and genealogies but also that insofar as they constitute material objects which have emerged from a particular society and cultural moment, they can be challenged, reworked or responded to by subsequent generations of writers through imitation, parody, critique, allusion or any other process of transposition and transformation.

The continuing relevance of notions of influence and of literary genealogy in a broad sense is suggested by Pope (2005), who traces the history of ideas about creative production from classical times to the present. While pointing to the different ways in which inspiration has been constructed through time – from divine inspiration to inspiration by another – he brings into alignment notions of inspiration and influence, showing that in the etymological sense of 'flowing into', rather than the more particular sense of 'sources, models and exemplars' (Pope, 2005, p. 91), the two concepts have a degree of overlap: a writer's work may show evidence of the impact of the work of another or of others on its production. Indeed, insofar as intertextuality may be understood as the absorption and transformation of one text by another, it too posits a view of creation and creativity which sees it as dependent on prior production, though in this case, notions of subjectivity and conscious agency on the part of the writer give way to the inevitability of textual transmission and the creation of networks of linguistic and cultural relations.

As Hutcheon (2006) points out, there is a kind of cultural paradox at work in contemporary society whereby adaptations are on the increase; yet there appears to remain suspicion that they are somewhat derivative rather than original and interesting works in their own right. Hutcheon (2006) attributes this paradox to the fact that adaptations are seen to be least risky in difficult economic times, since they are often based on 'original' works that have been tried and tested. The pleasure, she argues, which is derived from adaptation relates to 'repetition with variation' (p. 4). Yet what she calls a (post)-Romantic bias is at work today tending to value the original creation over anything produced by its adapters, despite the fact that many 'original' artists have acknowledged their debt to prior sources. She draws a parallel here with the role of translators who traditionally have been seen as simply transferring content from one language to another rather than as creators in their own right, though she also acknowledges that such views are changing under the influence of translators and writers like Bassnett (2002) who stress the transformative nature of translation and other kinds of textual production.

Drawing on notions of transformation and translation, I shall seek to demonstrate in this chapter the extent to which writers depend on prior production and in fact use it as a basis for the production of new works. If I refer to this process as transformation and translation rather than adaptation, it is for a number of reasons. First, in line with the view taken throughout this book, I wish to emphasize the commonalities between (creative) writing and translation in a broad sense; second, I wish to acknowledge the interdependence of textual entities which dialogue with and speak to one another (cf. Kristeva, 1986 and Bakhtin, 2004). Third, I wish to highlight the fact that these processes are part and parcel of creative production per se and not just a by-product of particular types of artistic endeavour such as an explicit adaptation from one medium to another. As will be seen, this chapter focuses on writers whose work is influenced by the work of other writers. In the case of the writers studied, there is a measure of self-consciousness and explicitness about their debt to or acknowledgement of the particular work and/or writer. However, I would contend that what is at issue is less the degree of explicitness on the part of a writer and more the extent to which there is evidence of textual affinities between the structures and themes of one work and those of another/others.

I shall begin by outlining Winterson's view of art, discussing in particular her evaluation of Woolf's *Orlando* before going on to examine structural and thematic parallels between *Orlando* and Winterson's *Sexing the Cherry*. I shall then go on to discuss what might be seen as a more complex case of translation and transformation by virtue of its contextual and cultural constraints, that of Ali Smith's *Girl Meets Boy* in relation to its various sources and influences, including Ovid's *Metamorphoses*.

A Writer's View of Literary Art: Winterson on Woolf

While contemporary writers may not use the language of literary theory or criticism, some do declare their sources of inspiration and allegiances and appear to be conscious of those writers and texts which in various ways seep into their psyche and alter their view of the world. Jeanette Winterson, for example, talks about what she calls 'strong texts' (Winterson, 1995, p. 26), that is, those which affect her deeply and cause her to redefine herself and her world. 'Strong texts', she writes, 'work along the borders of our minds and alter what already exists' (p. 26). In Part Two of *Art Objects*, a book of essays on literature and the question of what constitutes literary art, Winterson devotes two chapters to Virginia Woolf. This is evidence of her acknowledgement of Woolf as a writer of strong texts, texts which served to transform the literary culture of her own time as well as having proved a source of inspiration for writers since, including, as we shall see, Winterson herself.

Interestingly, Part Two is entitled 'Transformation' and sets out Winterson's artistic credo. She sees literature as having a reality separate from life; as such art does not offer direct access to either the writer's life nor to her psychology. She goes further when she writes that 'the intersection of a writer's life and a writer's work is irrelevant to the reader' (p. 27), a position likely to be contested by those for whom the facts of (auto-)biography or a writer's social and cultural location may be seen to shed light on the writer's work, even where no one-to-one correspondence is adduced. By contrast, Winterson's view of literary art seeks to emphasize the process of transformation by which language is heightened and events and states of affairs are transposed from their 'ordinary' context and 'carried above the literalness of life' (Winterson, 1995, p. 66).

Woolf's *Orlando*

Winterson characterizes Woolf's *Orlando*, (first published in 1928) in the following, rather telegraphic terms: '*Orlando* is metaphor, is transformation, is art' (p. 66). By this she means to assert its status as an artfully produced text and carefully controlled piece of language which challenges expectations, while delighting in its construction of a world sufficient onto itself.

> When Woolf is read and taught, she needs to be read and taught as a poet; she is not a writer who uses for words things, for her, words are things, incantatory, substantial. In her fiction, her polemic is successful because it is subordinated to the right of spells. (p. 70)

Winterson goes on to outline the characteristics and thematic interests of *Orlando*, as she sees them. Clearly, in terms of transformation *Orlando* is a novel all about the 'transformation of sex and sexuality' (67) in that it relates the supposed biography of its main protagonist, Orlando, from the sixteenth- to the twentieth century, documenting along the way the various changes (in sex, in location, both geographic and historical) that befall the character, who despite his/her longevity and sexual transformation is recognizably the same in terms of interests, character traits and even outward appearance – 'their faces remained, as their portraits prove, practically the same' (Woolf, 1993, p. 87).

These transformations, according to Winterson, are skilfully realized both through the language used, 'at once delicate and audacious' (Winterson, 1995, p. 70), and through its appeal to the reader to accept 'an invitation to believe' (p. 71) or perhaps to suspend her disbelief for the duration of a book that offers 'an immediate challenge to conventional genre-boxing' (p. 71) by consciously playing with the conventions of biography with its expectation of an account of a life based on documentary evidence and verifiable facts, and the world of fantasy which gives much freer rein to the imagination. For the world Woolf describes 'is an invented history, with certain key facts to support her imagination, but the reader should be wary of *Orlando*'s facts' (p. 72). Winterson is alluding here to Woolf's playfulness in *Orlando* and the fact that she uses her knowledge of reader expectations to subvert convention while continuing to carry her reader along with her.

Woolf is aware, for example, that the passage where Orlando is transformed from male to female is likely to stretch the bounds of plausibility in this apparently true account of a life. In the lead-up to this passage, she has on numerous occasions shown the role of biographer to be a more treacherous and contentious one than might be imagined, since there are likely to be episodes in people's lives where the available evidence is scant and where the biographer is forced to fill in from fragments a plausible account of events. In preparing to reveal Orlando's change of sex, she skilfully manipulates reader expectation by recognizing the biographer's dilemma and using it as a means of continuing her story.

> Would that we might here take the pen and write Finis to our work! Would that we might spare the reader what is to come and say to him in so many words, Orlando died and was buried. But here, alas, Truth, Candour, and Honesty, the austere Gods who keep watch and ward by the inkpot of the biographer, cry No! Putting their silver trumpets to their lips they demand in one blast, Truth! And again they cry Truth! and (sic) sounding yet a third time in concert they peal forth, the Truth and nothing but the Truth! (Woolf, 1993, p. 84)

This playful engagement with the expected role and qualities of biographer, where expectations of truth-telling are set against, and indeed undermine, issues both of decorum and of plausibility, allows the narrative to continue by delivering the essential 'fact' of Orlando's change of sex, while continuing to pay lip service to the role of biographer. 'He stretched himself. He rose. He stood upright in complete nakedness before us, and while the trumpets pealed Truth! Truth! Truth! we have no choice but confess – he was a woman' (p. 87).

While in many ways *Orlando*, dedicated to Vita Sackville West, is atypical of Woolf's oeuvre, there are aspects of the book which reflect her deeply held concerns, concerns, for example, about the nature of reality and the passage of time and ideas about truth in art. Though playfully rendered, there is evidence of engagement with the difference between chronological and psychological time, between inner and outer realities. There is an extended passage on the nature of time and human perception of it in the context of a turning point in Orlando's life. For by the age of 30, Orlando has already amassed a great deal of experience of life, love, loss and disillusion. His Russian princess has left him and his literary efforts have been ridiculed in the poet Nick Greene's 'Visit to a Nobleman in the Country'. His life has been reduced to the two things he feels he can trust: 'dogs and nature; an elk-hound and a rose bush' (p. 58).

In reducing the expansiveness and complexity of life to two concrete objects, Woolf is not only gently mocking Orlando but is also by extension ridiculing the focus of some Realists on material objects at the expense of a kind of interiority. We know from Woolf's essay, first published in 1925, on 'Modern Fiction' that she felt that the materialists, as she called them, were somehow missing the point of fiction by focusing on the external trappings of life while failing to capture its spirit. Woolf's fiction, by contrast, is most concerned with capturing the subjective experience of life in all its fleetingness and ephemerality and of using methods appropriate to the spirit of a new age.

In relation to *Orlando*, Woolf plays with the role of biographer, musing on the problem of how to render an account of a period in her subject's life in which nothing startling or of much interest appears to have happened and where there is, at least superficially, a recurrence of the same events and activities: giving orders and doing the business of his vast estates (p. 59). Yet beneath the apparent regularity of time passing, there is another psychological reality where time is experienced rather differently.

An hour, once it lodges in the queer element of the human spirit, may be stretched to fifty or a hundred times its clock length; on the other hand, an hour may be accurately represented on the timepiece of the mind by one second. This extraordinary discrepancy between time on the clock and time in the mind is less known than it should be and deserves fuller invest-igation. (p. 59)

This recognition and discussion of the problematics of time and how it is experienced is a typical Woolfian theme, one which, as we shall see, is con-sciously picked up in Winterson's *Sexing the Cherry* (first published in 1989). Another related theme explored in *Orlando* and taken up in *Sexing the Cherry* is that of the relationship between the inner and outer selves and the extent to which the self is singular and stable or multiple and potentially shifting over time and in response to new sets of circumstances. In portraying a character whose sex changes over time and whose life spans the best part of 400 years, Woolf has set up a dramatic situation that permits such questions to be explored, since the extent to which external changes in Orlando's situation generate or entail changes in character and behaviour naturally follow. As we will see, Winterson's main characters, the Dog Woman and Jordan, are also transmo-grified across time and reappear 300 years later in the guise of the (nameless) female protester against pollution camped out by the river and a naval cadet called Nicolas Jordan.

In respect of *Orlando*, I have already alluded to the commentary following the change of sex which maintains that Orlando's portraits show evidence of a remarkable resemblance over time (p. 87). There are passages, however, which indicate awareness on the part of Orlando of the behavioural con-sequences of this change of sex. Thus in the guise of a woman, Orlando comes to understand the differences between the sexes better and to experience the societal constraints and prohibitions that follow from her new position. Yet, there is a certain ambiguity in her position as a woman who knows what it was like to have been a man: 'and indeed, for the time being, she seemed to vacillate; she was man; she was woman; she knew the secrets, shared the weak-nesses of each' (p. 100).

Later in the novel, however, subtle changes in demeanour and behaviour are made apparent. This gives rise to a discussion of the role and importance of clothes in shaping behaviour and leads to consideration of Orlando's apparent 'vacillation from one sex to the other' (p. 121). For she seemed to combine male and female attributes in her person and to evidence now male, now female patterns of behaviour. The biographer at this point concludes: 'Whether, then, Orlando was most man or woman, it is difficult to say and cannot now be decided' (p. 122). Yet as we reach the mid-nineteenth century Orlando herself reflects on how, despite all these changes, 'she had remained [. . .] fundamentally the same. She had the same brooding meditative character, the same love of animals and nature, the same passion for the country and the seasons' (p. 153).

By the time we reach the twentieth century, the matter of sex returns again in relation to the outcome of lawsuits initiated in Orlando's absence from her estates. She is pronounced to be female with any future male heirs to inherit the estates after her death. This is pertinent insofar as she marries Marmaduke Bonthrop Shelmerdine, who spends most of his time navigating Cape Horn, and gives birth to a son. Her relations with Shelmerdine give rise to further discussion of male and female characteristics with the eventual acknowledgement that in each sex there may reside a combination of both masculine and feminine attributes. The sympathy which exists between Orlando and Shelmerdine is such as to make them doubt the sex of the other: 'You're a woman, Shel!', she cried. 'You're a man, Orlando!', he cried (Woolf, 1993, p. 164). These exclamations and doubts cast on the other's sex recur at intervals because of the degree of understanding they have of each other:

> For each was so surprised at the quickness of the other's sympathy, and it was to each such a revelation that a woman could be as tolerant and free-spoken as a man, and a man as strange and subtle as a woman, that they had to put the matter to the proof at once. (Woolf, 1993, p. 168)

What also comes to the fore here is Woolf's playfulness, which, along with the similarity in themes, is a characteristic of Winterson's *Sexing the Cherry*. While Winterson does not draw explicit attention to parallels with *Orlando*, her inclusion in *Art Objects* of two essays on Woolf is already a strong indicator of Woolf's importance to Winterson as a writer. Indeed Winterson is highly conscious of the need to acknowledge writers from the past and is aware of the literary benefits to be reaped:

> A writer uninterested in her lineage is a writer who has no lineage. The slow gestations and transformations of language are my proper study and there can be no limit on that study. I cannot do new work without known work. (Winterson, 1995, p. 172)

The choice of the word 'gestations' is an interesting one insofar as it acknowledges the slow process of giving birth to a work, a work carried within you for some time. In conjunction with the notion of 'transformations', a term to which Winterson returns again and again, there is clear acknowledgement of the general principles by which a work is created, that is from the seed of other works. I do not wish to suggest that *Sexing the Cherry* has no other sources and influences but Woolf – that is clearly not the case – but I would argue that the thematic and material similarities with Woolf's *Orlando* are striking. Indeed, there are a number of images which, as we shall see, permeate both works above and beyond what might be termed the 'psychic continuity' (Scott, 2000, p. 94) evident in Winterson's reworking and transformation of Woolf's novel.

Writing as Transformation: Winterson's *Sexing the Cherry*

Sexing the Cherry is a novel about transformation in a number of senses. There are the changes that take place over time in people and in their circumstances and environments; and there are the stories and histories that are relayed through time and which are subject to transposition and transformation in the process of being retold and rewritten. That Winterson is aware of the fact that these processes of transformation are effected in ways that are not always subject to laws of exactness and precision is evidenced in commentary embedded in *Sexing the Cherry* itself. For example, in relating Fortunata's story – Fortunata being one of the dancing princesses and object of one of the main character's attention – we read that 'transformation from one element to another [. . .] is a process that cannot be documented. It is fully mysterious. No one really knows what effects the change [. . .] We can only guess at what happened' (Winterson, 2001, p. 131).

The passage just quoted is of interest in a number of respects. As a story within a story within a story in *Sexing the Cherry*, where Fortunata is explaining why she is in the service of Artemis, it is a commentary first on the transformations effected in mythology and within the human psyche. Second, it relates to the speculative nature of process in relation to the constituent elements of product. Third, it can be seen as a commentary on storytelling itself whereby a tale, comprising one set of characters and events, is metamorphosed in the spaces of imagination into another which resembles but does not reproduce it. Fourthly, if we think back to the anxieties of the biographer in *Orlando* in relation to episodes which appear to defy rational explanation, seem implausible or 'dark, mysterious and undocumented' (Woolf, 1993, p. 38), it is difficult not to hear in Winterson's novel an echo of the same playfulness and to see in Winterson's interest in imaginative realities 'sufficiently at odds with our daily reality to startle us out of it' (Winterson, 2001, p. 188), a continuation of Woolf's belief in the power of art to come closer to life as it is lived in the mind of an ordinary person on an ordinary day, that is to say, in all its diversity and incongruity.

As a writer Winterson is conscious of literature as 'energetic space' (Winterson, 2001, p. 178), a space constituted by one for whom fiction 'needs, more than ever, to remember itself as imaginative, innovative, Other' (p. 178) by engaging with works from the past and 'translating' them 'into a form that answers to twenty-first century needs' (p. 191). This, for Winterson, means that the conventional novel form is no longer an appropriate vehicle for writing

today. What is required is '[a] form that is not "a poem" as we usually understand the term, and not "a novel" as the term is defined by its own genesis'
(p. 191). What we need is a kind of poetic fiction rendered in a language that
is 'solid enough for its meaning and powered enough for its flight' (p. 167).
This is in essence what Winterson is trying to achieve and therefore it is perhaps
not by chance that she is drawn to Woolf's poetic prose and what she sees as
Woolf's associative method of making connections, 'which is a poet's method'
(Winterson, 2001, p. 74). Throughout *Art Objects* Winterson makes clear her
debt to the Modernists, including Woolf, praising in particular their concern
with fighting a war against 'cloudy language' and allowing 'images [to] multiply
out of the words themselves' (p. 74).

Like Woolf's Orlando, Winterson's *Sexing the Cherry* is a novel that spans
centuries and draws on the 'facts' of history to support the development of a
chronological frame. Unlike *Orlando*, where the focus is on the development
of the main character over an extended period of time, *Sexing the Cherry* is set
largely in the period from 1630 to 1665 and concerns the story of the Dog
Woman and her adopted son Jordan fished out of the Thames; however, there
are stories within stories which span a larger time frame and the latter part
of the novel entitled simply 'Some Years Later' appears to be set in the 1980s
and early 1990s. It features characters who in some senses are the modern
counterparts of the Dog Woman and Jordan, the former a young chemistry
graduate who has taken to camping by polluted rivers to draw attention to
environmental issues; the latter a navel cadet who seems to lack the ambition
of his friend Jack, an analyst in the city. At the end of the novel their paths
cross when Nicolas Jordan reads about the young environmentalist in the paper
and decides to seek her out.

Links between the two time frames are more complex than this, however.
Into the section entitled 'Some Years Later' is woven the continuing story of
the Dog Woman and Jordan following the Great Fire of London and Jordan's
return from a trip with Tradescant after which he presents a pineapple to the
King. Their traits and experiences dovetail with those of their contemporary
counterparts in a number of ways. On board ship one evening, Nicolas Jordan
hears a man's voice saying 'They are burying the King at Windsor today' and
when he looks round sees a man in strange clothes looking out over the water.
He seems to recognize him from somewhere; it is as if he has fallen through a
black hole and time has collapsed. Above him, he hears a bird cry, Tradescant
sighs at his side, and he has become Jordan. Likewise, the chemistry graduate,
who has had a weight problem in the past, imagines herself to be 'huge, raw, a
giant' (Winterson, 2001, p. 121). Reminiscent of the Dog Woman, who collects
the eyeballs and teeth of Puritans in a sack, she imagines herself roaming the
world with a sack filling it up with executives from the City and military men
from the Pentagon whom she takes on a tour of the butter mountains, wine
lakes and grain silos, showing them the world's inequalities and enrolling them
on courses in feminism and ecology.

These parallels in interests and experiences serve to point to the inter-connectedness of things and people over time. Just as in *Orlando* there were passages on the nature of memory and the difference between chronological time and our psychological experience of it, there are passages in *Sexing the Cherry* on the nature of time. These passages reinforce a view of the world where time is relative rather than absolute and emphasize the possibility of the co-existence of past, present and future. The view of time articulated by Jordan has much in common with ideas about time considered by the biographer in Woolf's text.

> Thinking about time is to acknowledge two contradictory certainties: that our outward lives are governed by the seasons and the clock; that our inward lives are governed by something much less regular – an imaginative impulse cutting through the dictates of daily time, and leaving us free to ignore the boundaries of here and now and pass like lightning along the coil of pure time, that is, the circle of the universe and whatever it does or does not contain. (Winterson, 2001, pp. 89–90)

The sentiments expressed in both Woolf and Winterson regarding the nature of time are remarkably similar. Both acknowledge the difference between seasonality and chronology on the one hand and man's experience of time on the other. A reminder of the beginning of the passage in Woolf makes this clear: 'But Time, unfortunately, though it makes animals and vegetables bloom and fade with amazing punctuality, has no such simple effect upon the mind of man' (Woolf, 1993, p. 59). Likewise, the focus on the difference between inner and outer realities is striking. In *Sexing the Cherry*, the passage on 'The Nature of Time' continues with an examination of our multiple selves as we move through time, changing in the process.

> The inward life tells us that we are multiple not single, and that our one existence is really countless existences holding hands like those cut-out paper dolls, but unlike the dolls never coming to an end. When we say, 'I have been here before,' perhaps we mean, 'I am here now,' but in another life, another time, doing something else. Our lives could be stacked together like plates on a waiter's hand. Only the top is showing, but the rest are there and by mistake we discover them. (Winterson, 2001, pp. 90–1)

What is particularly striking when we compare this to a passage in *Orlando*, also dealing with changes in self over time, is the inclusion in *Sexing the Cherry* of an image unmistakably borrowed from Woolf:

> For if there are (at a venture) seventy-six different times all ticking in the mind at once, how many different people are there not – Heaven help us – all having lodgment at one time or another in the human spirit? Some say two

thousand and fifty two. So that it is the most usual thing in the world for a person to call, directly they are alone, Orlando? (if that is one's name) meaning by that, Come, come! I'm sick to death of this particular self. I want another [. . .] Orlando? still the Orlando she needs may not come; *these selves of which we are built up, one on top of another, as plates are piled on a waiter's hand*, have attachments elsewhere [. . .] (Woolf, 1993, p. 201; italics added for emphasis)

The material similarity of some of the images in Woolf and Winterson, such as the one above, as well as the fact that they are embedded in similar contexts and reflect an interest in similar themes provides evidence of dialogue – 'a voice answering a voice' (Woolf, 1993, p. 213) – and engagement across time of one writer with another. Not that Winterson has ever sought to deny her interest in Woolf; on the contrary, she has in the past depicted herself as an heir to Woolf, while acknowledging in *Art Objects* that 'we cannot look for the new Virginia Woolf' (Winterson, 2001, p. 177) but must 'know what tradition is' (p. 177), understand the central place of Modernism within that and look for 'a fresh development of language' and 'new forms of writing' (p. 177). These new forms of writing come not out of a literary and cultural vacuum but emerge, as we have seen, in response to prior works or strong texts, as Winterson calls them, which demand engagement on the part of a new generation of writers.

Texts in Dialogue: A View of Creative Production

In the course of this chapter, I have been arguing a view of creative production that assumes that writers are first and foremost responsive readers of text and that their own productions are shaped materially and thematically, to a greater or lesser extent, by the 'influence' of particular texts upon them. As part of material culture, works of literature, like other textual products, bear witness to what has gone into their production, though, as we have seen, this does not mean that one text is a copy or reproduction of another; nor is it always the case that the various influences are easy to untangle. However, discussion of the thematic commonalities and in some instances the very imagery used in *Orlando* and *Sexing the Cherry* has served to demonstrate the interdependence of textual artefacts and to provide evidence, both textual and documentary, of the creative potential of a dialogue with writers of the past and of the way in which literary cultures are transformed over time.

Indeed, as Winterson has stated, it is impossible for writers not to take account of their literary lineage and the language of their forebears. In this sense, what 'flows in' from one work to another is generative of new works as well as new interpretations of previous works. Such a view of creation and creativity sees it as necessarily dependent on what has gone before and acknowledges the role of the material constituents of a culture, including its language/s, and available generic forms and conventions, in the production of new work. This is not to diminish the status or quality of what has been produced, nor to deny the sometimes unconscious creative impulses of writers. It is, however, aimed at pointing to the fact that innovation can stem from deliberate engagement with writers from the past. This, as we shall see, is true of Ali Smith's (2007) reworking of the myth of Iphis in *Girl Meets Boy*.

Ali Smith's *Girl Meets Boy*: Context of Production

The Canongate Myths Series is a venture begun by a commercial publishing house with the aim of commissioning contemporary writers to choose an ancient myth and rewrite it in such a way as to be of interest and relevance to a twenty-first-century audience. To date, 12 volumes have appeared, beginning in 2005, with works by writers as various as Margaret Atwood, Jeanette Winterson, Alexander McCall Smith, Philip Pullman and Ali Smith. Clearly, the project's very rationale presupposes an acquaintance with and response to a version of a myth from the past and its retelling in a form likely to grab and hold the attention of a contemporary audience. There is, in this instance, no denying a source text (ST) or series of source texts which form the basis of the production of a new work, or what we might call target text (TT), which is supposed to bear some kind of relation to the 'original' yet appeal to a modern readership. However, as we shall see, the apparently simple question of sources and influences turns out to be more complex than we might have supposed in this instance.

For the very substance of ancient myths is available in a number of translations and versions, supposing, of course, that the Canongate authors have not read their myth in the original Greek or Latin text. In the case of the myth of Iphis, chosen by Ali Smith, as a kind of base narrative for the production of her new work *Girl Meets Boy*, the situation is complicated by the fact that Ovid's *Metamorphoses*, Book IX of which Smith acknowledges to be the source of the myth which she reworks, is itself a text dependent on a reworking of ancient Greek myths. As Pope (2005, p. 155) points out: '[A]ll the myths and stories Ovid recounts were far from original with him: all had circulated in some shape or form – often many – before'. The point Pope is making, and one on which I am picking up and extending to the present case, is that Ovid was himself creating something new from a retelling of stories that were part and parcel of the cultural inheritance of his time. Pope is not denying Ovid's ability to transform what he read and imbibed in new and interesting ways. Indeed, he speaks of his ' "genius" for *re . . . creation*' and praises the 'skilled and spirited adaptation that his writing has encouraged' (Pope, 2005, p. 156; italics in original). It is in this same spirit of skilled and lively adaptation (in a non-technical sense) that I wish to examine Smith's creative response to her Canongate brief and to look at the ways in which she has chosen to transform the material culturally available to her using the resources at her disposal.

Girl Meets Boy: The Metamorphosis of an Old Story

The blurb on the inside cover of the hardback edition of the book (Smith, 2007) and on the Canongate Myths Series website gives an inkling of the tenor and general import of Smith's take on Ovid:

> Girl meets boy. It's a story as old as time. But what happens when an old story meets a brand new set of circumstances?
>
> Ali Smith's re-mix of Ovid's most joyful metamorphosis is a story about the kind of fluidity that can't be bottled and sold.
>
> It is about girls and boys, girls and girls, love and transformation, a story of puns and doubles, reversals and revelations.
>
> Funny and fresh, poetic and political, Girl meets boy is a myth of metamorphosis for the modern world (http://www.themyths.co.uk/?p=15)

There are a number of elements of the description and evaluation that require comment. First, there is the notion that an old story, such as what might be expected to happen when a girl meets a boy, can be given new life in new circumstances. Second, the reader understands that Smith's fluid reworking of Ovid's tale introduces some novel elements, elements which we will only come to appreciate, once we've read the work and compared it to Ovid's version but we know already that it has been updated such that it is considered 'a myth of metamorphosis for the modern world'. To read *Girl Meets Boy*, if one is not familiar with the substance of Ovid's *Metamorphoses* (Book IX), is to enjoy a tale of lesbian and heterosexual love in a setting which appears to share some of the characteristics of a recognizable social world in the early twenty-first century – international corporations; creative gurus; commodification and the marketing of natural resources; graffiti artists – but which at the same time evidences aspects which sit awkwardly within a realist narrative frame (e.g. changes in gender; expansive time frames), not to mention the element of playfulness, parody and social satire. The latter relates not so much to Ovid or the myth of Iphis but rather to the language of advertising and to a world where everything, including the imagination, can apparently be bottled and sold.

For this is a tale which takes the bare bones of Ovid – a story of love between two girls and its happy resolution – and transforms it into a love story spun on the thread of the myth of Iphis into a larger thematic web. For Smith embeds the elements of the tale, told and retold by one of the characters, Robin Goodman, to her lover Anthea Gunn, into what might be deemed a critique of modern enterprise culture and of the commercial appropriation of creativity. Robin comes to Anthea's attention while the latter is working, somewhat reluctantly at her sister's behest, at Pure, an international conglomerate, a subsidiary of which is focused on bottled water. It is Robin who is arrested for defacing company property by writing on the Pure sign in protest at the company's making money out of a natural resource. She adds her signature to the words of protest, a signature which Anthea first reads as Iphisol and later learns to be Iphis07. Anthea leaves the Tuesday Creative Lecture, where Keith has been leading the team in coming up with a new name for Scottish bottled water, to go and see what all the fuss is about outside and finds herself drawn to the beautiful boy-girl or girl-boy she sees up the ladder completing her handiwork 'with a series of arrogant and expert slants and curlicues' (Smith, 2007, p. 44).

Shortly afterwards, Robin and Anthea embark on a relationship and it is in them that we have a modern-day Iphis and Ianthe. That this is so is made explicit when towards the end of the novel both are arrested for writing messages all over town about the inequalities and injustices they wish to bring to public attention. They sign themselves off as Iphis and Ianthe, adding 'the message girls 2007' in some cases, 'the message boys 2007' in others, in recognition perhaps of the fluidity of gender and as if to confirm or echo an earlier conversation on the subject of Ovid and the fact that as a writer he knows, 'more than most, that the imagination doesn't have a gender' (Smith, 2007, p. 97).

This conversation comes in the section entitled 'Us' when Robin and Anthea have got together and are swapping life histories and stories. Anthea has revealed that she had tried to find out about Robin on the basis of her signature, which she misread, wondering who Iphisol might be; Robin laughs at her mistake, corrects her and recounts a version of the myth of Iphis for her benefit. Her first account, at approximately a page and a half, is a synopsis of the Iphis story as recounted by Ovid (approximately 9 pages in Penguin translation). It contains an outline of the events leading up to the marriage of Iphis and Ianthe after the intervention of the goddess Isis such that the girl Iphis is transformed into a boy and is thus able to go through with what might otherwise have been a tricky marriage. The focus of interest in this version is principally the resolution of a dilemma on the night before the wedding. There is little reference to the circumstances surrounding Iphis's birth and her life as a girl raised as a boy nor is her frustration at the possibility of not being able to please her bride dwelt upon.

The second time the tale is told it is in recognition of the fact that tales are usually spun out, embellished and delivered in accordance with the context of utterance and the expectations and needs of the listener. In this second version, the teller is interrupted by the listener and the tale is more dynamic as the listener reacts to what she hears. In this sense, it is more like a naturally occurring conversation than a monologic tale delivered as a piece and without interruption. Robin has scarcely begun with an indication of time and setting – 'A long time ago on the island of Crete' (Smith, 2007, p. 88) – before Anthea declares, 'I've been there! We went there [. . .] We had a holiday there when we were kids' (p. 88) and proceeds to recount an incident from the holiday. Robin begins again in a more elaborate way, building into her account aspects of what Anthea has told her and using them to better situate the tale she wishes to tell.

> A long time ago, Robin said, long before motorbike hire, long before motors, long before bikes, long before you, long before me, back before the great tsunami that flattened most of northern Crete and drowned most of the Minoan cities, which, by the way, was probably the incident responsible for the creation of the myth about the lost city of Atlantis. (Smith, 2007, pp. 88–9)

But she is interrupted again, as Anthea reacts to Robin's own digression regarding the creation of the myth of Atlantis. This provides Anthea with the opportunity to respond by talking about the role of myth within society, a topic clearly of relevance to the story as a whole, but not of particular relevance at this point. However, the reader understands the interruption and commentary to be serving as a kind of meta-text in relation to one of the other strands of Smith's novel – the role of advertising in society – as well as providing a thematic link connecting notions of cultural transmission and transformation. One can even see in Smith's elaborate and digressive retelling of the myth a playful modelling of the process of creativity which proceeds by association and the making of connections between the given and the new.

In frustration at the multiple interruptions, Robin asks whether Anthea wants to hear the story or not and only proceeds when she is certain she has Anthea's attention. The tale then proceeds with commentary on both sides. For example, picking up on the fact that in Ovid's version Ligdus, father of Iphis, comes to his wife and wishes her an easy delivery before indicating that if she gives birth to a girl, rather than a boy, the child will have to be killed because of the economic burden which girls impose, Robin portrays Telethusa as responding sarcastically to her husband's concern about the painlessness of the delivery and has her reply: 'Hmm, right [. . .] That's likely, isn't it?' (Smith, 2007, p. 90). But she goes on to acknowledge that she is 'imposing far too modern a reading on it' and indicates that Telethusa 'acted correctly for her time' (p. 91). The narration of the tale is in this sense, self-conscious, as Robin incorporates different perspectives (i.e. ancient and modern) and different registers into her rendering of the story.

With respect to the second element, that in the event of giving birth to a girl, the child will have to be killed, there is another digression and commentary, in response to Anthea's remark 'Thank God we're modern' (p. 91). Robin goes on to point out that in some parts of the world girls are aborted; red or blue ink is used by doctors to indicate the sex of the unborn child so that parents can decide what to do. What these examples highlight is that as the tale is being told, its substance is being evaluated by both teller and listener, as they apply their modern understanding to an ancient myth and try to make sense of it in the light of contemporary concerns.

The language used by Robin to recount the tale veers between a kind of paraphrase of the original and a modern, very colloquial register. For example, in Robin's recount of the tale, Iphis stands in a field and shouts her frustration at the gods:

Why have you done this to me? You fuckers. You jokers. Look what's happened now. I mean, look at that cow there. What'd be the point in giving her a cow instead of a bull? I can't be a boy to my girl! I don't know how! I wish I'd never been born! You've made me wrong! I wish I'd been killed at birth! Nothing can help me! (Smith, 2007, p. 95)

In the Penguin translation (2004), Iphis expresses her frustration in a slightly different register:

Almost in tears, she sighed: 'Oh, what will become of me now?
I'm possessed by a love that no one has heard of, a new kind of passion,
a monstrous desire! If heaven had truly wanted to spare me,
it ought to have done so. If not, and the gods were out to destroy me,
they might at least have sent me some natural, normal affliction.
Cows never burn with desire for cows, nor mares for mares;
ewes are attracted to rams and every stag has his hind;
the same with the mating of birds. Throughout the animal kingdom
the female is never smitten with passionate love for a female.
I wish I had never been born a woman, I wish I were dead! (pp. 375–6)

The first obvious difference is the difference in length. Ali Smith's version is much shorter and does not contain the extended lament about Iphis's fate evident in the Penguin translation. However, the substance of the sentiment is expressed, albeit in rather more abbreviated form and in less elaborated language, and the order in which ideas and sentiments are delivered is broadly comparable.

Smith does not indicate the version of Ovid she used as source material; however, the point is not really to compare versions of the story in detail but rather to give a flavour of their register and thematic concerns. As I have tried to show, the context in which the Iphis myth is related in *Girl Meets Boy* already gives it new meaning by virtue of the fact that it is embedded in a contemporary story, some elements of which seem very far away from Ovid. However, the spirit of Ovid hovers over the novel insofar as it deals with questions of the fluidity of gender and the transformative power of love. By virtue of the embedding of the story within another story, different narrative levels are created, which permit the establishment of new relations and new connections between different discourses and sets of events. More concretely, this means that above and beyond the thematic links already articulated, there is the possibility of critique and commentary, of dialogue between past and present, between one set of circumstances and another.

Elsewhere I have elaborated the way in which Smith borrows the rhetorical structure of a talk by a French sociologist and uses it to great effect in the construction of a speech by Keith, Pure's creative guru (Doloughan, 2009). Smith also acknowledges drawing on books dealing with the corporate theft of the world's natural resources, in this case principally water. Her engagement with these texts is also apparent in *Girl Meets Boy*. Here, however, my focus is on the role of the Ovidian myth in helping to shape Smith's text. One of the things I have been suggesting is that the recounting of the myth in *Girl Meets Boy* is structured in such a way as to permit commentary on it from a modern perspective. Thus, for example, Anthea suggests that perhaps Ianthe '*wants a girl* [. . .]. Clearly Iphis is exactly the kind of boy-girl or girl-boy she loves' (p. 95), opening the myth up to a different interpretation or a different kind of resolution. As Robin's response shows, she is aware of that possibility but indicates that it's not 'in the original story' (p. 95).

Robin continues her narration of the story stopping at the point where Iphis is wondering what to do. She asks Anthea what she thinks is going to happen, thereby drawing her further into the dialogic construction of the narrative.

> Well, she's going to need some help. The father's not going to be any good [. . .] And Ianthe thinks that's what a boy is, what Iphis is [. . .] So. It's either the mother or the goddess. (Smith, 2007, p. 98)

For the myth to be of interest to Anthea, as listener, and Robin, as teller, it has to engage them and help progress the dynamic of their own evolving relationship, as well as 'speak to' the broader themes of the novel. It manages to do this through what might be termed its deconstruction and reconstruction of the myth and through its participatory mode of delivery such that the reader learns more about Robin and Anthea along the way. It's a kind of dramatic re-enactment and creative transformation of the tale within the frame of another, thematically linked story. It also employs humour in relation, for example, to Iphis's physical transformation from girl to boy.

> Jaw lengthens, stride lengthens, absolutely everything lengthens. By the time she'd got home, the girl Iphis had become exactly the boy that she and her girl needed her to be. And the boy their two families needed. And everyone in the village needed. And all the people coming from all over the place who were very anxious to have a really good party needed. (Smith, 2007, p. 99)

Compare the more circumspect way in which the transformation is articulated in the Penguin translation (2004):

> [. . .] and Iphis followed behind her (Telethusa) with longer strides than she normally took. Her girlish complexion had lost its whiteness, her limbs grew stronger, and even her features sharpened. Her bandless hair seemed

cut to a shorter length. She'd felt a new vigour she'd never enjoyed as the female she'd been 'til a moment before. That female was now transformed to a male! (pp. 378–9)

Apart from the two recounts of the Iphis myth which have just been discussed, there is reference to it once again in the final section entitled 'All together now' which relates the story's happy ending or more precisely several versions of it. This section is built around the wedding between Iphis and Ianthe (aka Robin and Anthea). In the Ovidian version, little detail of the wedding day is given but here Smith constructs a wedding from fragments of various texts both ancient and modern. For example, the section begins: 'Reader, I married him/her', clearly an allusion to the double wedding at the end of Jane Austen's *Pride and Prejudice*. There are also references to Sappho's poems (cf. poem 65) on the theme of marriage (e.g. 'we raised high the roofbeams, carpenters, for there was no other bride, o bridegroom, like her' (p. 149)). Indeed, the final section is a kind of consciously spun intertextual weave. It brings into a dynamic relationship fragments of works of the past and the newly formed elements of the present work. The textual interplay of ancient and modern which it evidences is celebratory and playful with a piling up of expressions, old and new, used to signal marriage and commitment (pp. 149–51).

At the wedding party, the newly-weds meet a 'beautiful Greek couple' (p. 155) who invite them to spend their honeymoon in Crete, which they duly do and stand on the site 'where the Iphis story had originated' (p. 156). Meanwhile back at the wedding party, the band strikes up and we have a detailed description of the entertainment, before the narrative breaks off again: 'Uh-huh.Okay. I know. In my dreams. What I mean is [. . .]' (p. 159) and we get a new version of events, followed by a commentary on the art and act of transformation. The narrator wonders what happens 'when things come together [. . .] or a story from then meets a story from now' (p. 160). There is affirmation towards the end of the novel of the continuity and subsistence of things through and over time and discussion of the process whereby one thing is made out of another:

and into another, and nothing lasts, and nothing's lost, and nothing ever perishes, and things can always change, because things will always change, and things will always be different, because things can always be different. (Smith, 2007, p. 160)

Metamorphosis then is depicted as a natural state of affairs; stories will continue to be told, because they need to be told, and are changed in the telling. And in the telling, we too change. Out of the possible constraints imposed by retelling an ancient myth for a contemporary audience, Smith manages to create a new story which borrows from Ovid material which is then restructured and reshaped into a different configuration. While Smith's text owes its genesis to Ovid's eighth-century poem, it becomes a novel for the twenty-first century through a process of creative transformation.

Conclusion

That the novel form is pliable and adaptable is confirmed by Pope (2005, p. 218; italics in the original) who indicates that 'novels have always tended to be radically *hybrid* in their origins and richly *heteroglossic* in the "varied voices" that they draw together'. Certainly, the present chapter has shown the extent to which new novelistic production is dependent on a reworking of strong texts from the past by contemporary writers conscious both of their literary lineage and of the need to push the boundaries of what has gone before and move in a new direction. This seeming contradiction between familiarity with a literary tradition and the ability to create new forms for new times is simply an acknowledgement of the fact that writers are responsive and imaginative readers who recognize that 'genres and forms are never fixed and finished but are subject to constant transformation' (Pope, 2005, p. 217). They use the material provided by their prior reading experience as a resource for the construction of a new work, a work marked by 'many voices, many connections' (Winterson, 1995, p. 180). As Winterson so aptly puts it: 'Art is metaphor. Metaphor is transformation' (p. 66).

Chapter 6

Narratives of Travel and Travelling Narratives

Introduction

In looking at what appear to be the characteristics of contemporary narrative, one of the arguments made in preceding chapters has related to increased interest in the affordances of the visual in otherwise verbal narratives and in concepts of narrative space. This has both a literal and a metaphoric dimension insofar as some narratives (e.g. Sebald's *Austerlitz*) are using visual means (diagrams, photos, reproductions of paintings etc.) to complement, progress and/ or undermine the verbal narrative or are operating through a close interaction of visual and verbal modes (e.g. Gaiman and McKean's *Signal to Noise*). Concomitant with this is a critical revaluation of the ability of words to cue or trigger images (cf. Herman, 2002) and renewed interest in the spaces of reading and of the imagination (Scott, 2006) as well as concern with the concept of reading path (cf. Kress, 2003). In short, while traditional definitions of narrative have emphasized aspects of temporality and changes over time in a character's mentality or in a state of affairs, contemporary narrative interest is more likely to be focused on the implications of a disruption or suspension of the temporal order and the effects of spatialization on narrative progression.

In this connection it is instructive to reflect on Augé's (2008) work on supermodernity and specifically what he refers to as non-places. By supermodernity, Augé means to point to changes in the contemporary cultural and anthropological landscape and to a move away from the concerns of modernity, which he sees as characterized by the co-existence of past and present, to the arrival of supermodernity, which is characterized by what he calls temporal and spatial excess and the return of individuality. 'Everything proceeds as if space had been trapped by time, as if there were no history other than the last forty-eight hours of news, from the inexhaustible stock of an unending history in the present' (Augé, 2008, p. 84). Not only has the grand narrative of history been collapsed into a series of little narratives or more recent newsworthy events relayed in short cycles but space too has become dependent on a series of relational, transport and communication networks. By means of the internet, mobile phones and other communication technologies, space seems to have been compressed insofar as we can communicate across vast distances and temporal zones. Travel, too, has been made easier and formerly distant places have become accessible through the availability of transport, which permits great distances to be traversed in comparatively little time.

In addition, the particularity of place has been replaced by the lack of specificity attached to notions of space, including outer and inner space. Unlike places which have a particular historical and geographical location, Augé sees non-places as representative of the contemporary era, those indeterminate and vaguely homogeneous spaces through which we pass without stopping or in which we are in transit, spaces such as motorways or airport lounges. He also refers to the spaces that are evoked by words and that have a virtual existence: 'the imagination of a person who has never been to Tahiti or Marrakesh takes flight the moment these names are read or heard' (Augé, 2008, p. 76). This evocation, triggered by a word, may in turn rely on the power of the image insofar as it relates to the sometimes rather generic and stereotypical images disseminated in travel guides and/or brochures, for example. Such an 'invasion of space by text' (p. 80) can also be seen in big supermarkets through which the shopper moves, largely in silence, reading labels, weighing fruit and vegetables and handing over payment, after everything has been electronically scanned. S/he may not even need to interact with the person at the checkout but has the option of self-service. Space-time configurations in the age of supermodernity are therefore decidedly different to those of modernity.

The relevance of this move from modernity to supermodernity and of the proliferation of non-spaces, as articulated by Augé, may not be immediately apparent in the context of a chapter on 'Narratives of Travel and Travelling Narratives'. However, as will be seen, in relation to the two works under study, Alain de Botton's *The Art of Travel* and Ben Okri's *In Arcadia*, the focus is on changing concepts of time and space, and their intersection, as they appear to be articulated and inscribed in narrative today. In what follows, my concern, broadly speaking, will be twofold: there will be consideration of the extent to which concepts of narrative change as they travel across boundaries, be they disciplinary, generic, cultural or geographic; there will also be consideration of the extent to which concern with questions of space have superseded a focus on time in narrative.

Clearly, in relation to the concept of travel, there are a number of relevant dimensions. Travel relates to mobility, in the sense of movement from one place to another; it also relates to temporality insofar as travel tends to take place in and over time. In addition, travel can be metaphoric rather than literal: ideas and customs, as well as people and goods, can travel and travel may take place in the world of actuality or in the world of imagination. The journey, in all its aspects, may, therefore, be seen as protypical of narrative in relation to both form and content, since it is concerned with movement in and progression over time on the part of a protagonist located within a particular world.

The Art of Travel and *In Arcadia* will be used to illustrate different dimensions of travel and to point to differences between place and space. From the perspective of tendencies in narrative today, they will be shown to be concerned with border crossing, both literal and metaphoric, and with the enactment of stylistic, thematic and organizational choices which accentuate the spatial dimensions of text by disrupting or seeming to suspend the temporal. These works may be seen as narratives of supermodernity insofar as they are structured around journeys but seem preoccupied with non-places and liminal spaces.

In the case of *The Art of Travel*, de Botton will be seen to focus on the 'two complementary but distinct realities' designated by the word 'non-place', that is 'spaces formed in relation to certain ends (transport, transit, commerce, leisure) and the relations that individuals have with these spaces' (Augé, 2008, p. 76). This will include fascination with the motorway and service station; and the airport terminal and departure lounge. It will also be concerned with the spaces of imagination triggered by words and images of places yet to be visited and/or imagined through the accounts of other writers and artists (e.g. Wordsworth's Lake District, Van Gogh's Provence). In this sense, de Botton is exploring the 'link between individuals and their surroundings in the space of non-place [which] is established through the mediation of words, or even texts' (Augé, 2008, p. 76).

With respect to *In Arcadia* what will be of interest in relation to this notion of supermodernity will be the focus on imaginary places and utopias perceived through text, both visual and verbal. As the band of misfits journeys by train from London to Paris and beyond in search of Arcadia (the lost ideal and the historical place), they are held together in a precarious balance through their shared identity as passengers, as they move through landscapes glimpsed through windows. As Augé (2008, p. 70) puts it, '[t]he traveller's space may thus be the archetype of *non-place*' (italics in original).

Alain de Botton's *The Art of Travel*

In *The Art of Travel* the author-narrator goes on a journey – indeed a series of journeys – as a result of which he comes to understand himself better. He also learns something about travel from a number of perspectives: personal, social and cultural. In addition, his conscious reading of place through the eyes of previous writers and travellers provides a structural mechanism for relating past to present and showing how vision, that is what we see, is a factor of what we have read, as well as of who we are. Narrative techniques, such as the presentation of multiple and intersecting storylines, are used and applied to 'layer' experience and to provide a critical and self-reflexive dimension. But this is not just a story about travel in a literal sense. It is also a work that journeys into the psyche and asks questions about human motivation and the pursuit of happiness. This 'in-built' philosophical, even didactic, impulse might seem at odds with a narrative impulse, narrowly construed.

For if narrative is equated with a particular dynamic – a plot-driven, episodic but ultimately coherent work – then de Botton's *The Art of Travel* appears less interested in plot and more interested in issues and lines of inquiry. At the same time, this is not a purely philosophical work. It has multiple interests: the whys and wherefores of travel; the cultural, social and psychological significance of travel; the dynamics of the quest (in this case for human happiness); the power of art and of landscape to open our eyes to new experiences and to mediate our vision of reality. Travel is treated as a multidimensional activity involving not just physical or geographic displacement but also potential changes in psychology or state of mind. It has a cultural history which, consciously or unconsciously, frames the endeavours of those who would travel, whether literally or metaphorically. The airport, the service station, the train and the plane are not simply places of arrival and departure and vehicles of transport. They are spaces where the codes of daily life and routine are somehow suspended; they offer the possibility of reflection, transformation and new departures. As de Botton (2003, p. 57) writes, '[j]ourneys are the midwives of thought. Few places are more conducive to internal conversations than a moving plane, ship or train.'

In this sense, movement is equated with border crossing and transgression and displacement with a suspension of normal codes of operation. The 'space' that travel opens up is a meditative one which allows the subject the leisure to contemplate what might otherwise get lost in the course of daily routine. Movement and stasis here are not mutually exclusive polar opposites but conditions of possibility for a journey through the mind. Like art, which selects what is to be shown and more or less consciously transforms the raw material with which it works, travel can permit a sharpening or refining of experience by providing the conditions necessary for reflexive thought. It can also free up or empty consciousness of self, opening up a space for the traveller to register things beyond himself.

Coming off the motorway and pulling into the service station might not immediately seem replete with poetic possibilities but among the neon lights, posters of food and passing motorists, de Botton experiences something akin to a poetry of place. What Augé (2008, p. 78) refers to as 'the innumerable "supports" (signboards, screens, posters) that form an integral part of the contemporary landscape' lead the tired motorist to the brightly lit haven of the self-service cafeteria where he is quickly and cheerfully processed before continuing his journey. The space he enters and through which he passes creates 'solitary contractuality' (Augé, 2008, p. 76), each motorist separate from the other, yet brought into a relation of similitude by virtue of the fact that they are all doing more or less the same things and have broken their journey for similar reasons. As Augé (2008, p. 83) puts it: 'The space of non-place creates neither singular identity nor relations; only solitude and similitude.'

The Art of Travel is described on de Botton's website (http://www.alaindebotton) in the following terms:

> The book mixes personal thought with insights drawn from some of the great figures of the past. Unlike existing guidebooks on travel, it dares to ask what the point of travel might be – and modestly suggests how we could learn to be less silently and guiltily miserable on our journeys.

Clearly, at one level this summary evaluation is aimed at enticing a prospective readership with its promise of something new: asking questions about the purposes and motivations of travel rather than simply talking about the sights and sounds of the journey. In addition, the fact that it sets personal insights in the context of ideas from writers and artists of the past is seen as a positive aspect of the book.

Whatever the context and primary function of the summary evaluation, it does point to some relevant design features of the book. For this is a book structured around the idea of a journey from departure to return (cf. section headings in the Contents page) – the trip to Barbados for some winter sun and subsequent return to a Britain that, unsurprisingly, has changed little in the interim. At the same time, the particular journey which frames and provides an overarching structure for a book concerned with the motivations as well as the mechanics of travel, generates or permits the inclusion of other trips taken by the author (e.g. to the Lake District, Amsterdam, Provence), trips taken in the footsteps of and evaluated against the grain of the insights and writings of other writers and artists. This is then a consciously self-reflexive and 'literary' book which reads current personal and societal concerns and interests in relation to the views and insights of past travellers and border crossers.

The work revolves around a character, Alain de Botton, who is also the narrator of the story. Because de Botton is also the named author on the cover of the book, it is tempting to assume that the autobiographical contract (Lejeune, 1982) is in force here and that therefore we can simply 'read off' aspects of the 'real' de Botton's life. However, as Korte (2008, p. 620) points out:

> [I]t is important to distinguish between author, narrating-I and experiencing-I, since the views voiced by the narrating-I might not be fully identical with those of the 'real' author, and the narrator may also, just like any first person narrator, create a certain distance from him or herself as traveller.

This distancing effect can be achieved, as in any narrative, by means of a disjunction between story-order and text-order (Rimmon-Kenan, 1983, p. 46), between the arrangements of events as they would have been ordered chronologically and the sequence in which they are recounted. By means of analepsis (the representation of events which happened in the past, relative to the story's present) and prolepsis (the representation of events which are yet to come in relation to story-order), it is possible to manipulate the presentation of events, thus indicating stance with respect to what has happened or what is yet to come from the perspective of the narrator's more experienced self. In addition, the technique of reading places through the works of other writers and artists (e.g. the Lake District through the eyes of Wordsworth, Provence through the eyes of Van Gogh) creates a layering of experience and a kind of spatio-temporal mediation with the possibility of an evaluation of what is lived and felt in the light of collective wisdom or relative to insights from the past. Aesthetic, as well as critical, effects may also be achieved through the application of a writerly and artistic lens to the representation of landscape and place.

In a review of some of de Botton's works, including *The Art of Travel*, Pulitzer prize-winning novelist Alison Lurie writes: 'the idea that prose might be both casual in manner and serious in intent is almost forgotten. It survives, however, in the work of Alain de Botton' (Lurie, 2007). She goes on to point to de Botton's 'aversion to deliberately difficult scholarly prose', indicating his early interest in the essayistic form in the style of Montaigne, one of his favourite authors. She notes, too, that de Botton's books were soon very 'openly presented as non-fiction' and that his reputation as a writer has been built on his ability to deal with serious issues in an accessible and informal, even popular, manner. Lurie's characterization of de Botton's work is of interest for a number of reasons. Her review points to the problems of categorization that have typified de Botton's work and his ability to cross genres (e.g. autobiography, biography, self-help manual) and create sometimes hybrid forms. It also indicates his preference for a form of writing – the essay – which allows for a philosophical treatment of issues from a personal perspective.

In the context of a book on *Contemporary Narrative*, the question arises of the contribution of de Botton's *The Art of Travel* to the issues already presented. To what extent, for example, can *The Art of Travel* be considered a narrative, given what has been said about de Botton's preference for the essayistic form and to what extent does de Botton's book fit the mould of travelogue or travel narrative? What I wish to show is that de Botton's book relies on a number of categorizations even as it critiques and transforms them. The seeming paradox of relying on a notion of genre while simultaneously subverting it from within or of mixing genres, thereby pointing to the limits of an idea of a 'pure' genre, is attended to by Derrida (1981, p. 60) in 'The Law of Genre'.

> Can one identify a work of art of whatever sort, but especially a work of discursive art, if it does not bear the mark of a genre, if it does not signal or mention it or make it remarkable in any way?

For Derrida the very hallmark of literature is that it expresses participation in a genre or genres while not necessarily belonging to that genre. It re-marks – in the dual sense of making/repeating a mark as well as bringing to notice or attention – its participation in a genre/s even as it signals its non-belonging.

A second point of relevance to the discussion made by Derrida in this same article relates to what he perceives to be confusion, reinforced by the Romantics, of 'mode' and 'genre'. The novel, for example, is generally treated as a genre with particular types of novel, such as the novel of education, considered as subgenres. The question then arises of the status of narrative and whether it is co-extensive with the novel or whether in fact, as a mode, it can be a property of any text. In talking therefore of travel narratives, it is important to bear in mind the potential for ambiguity. Is the term travel narrative intended to refer to a particular mode of storytelling, which happens to be about travel, or does it aim to designate a particular type of content, or both, on the assumption that it is possible to separate form and content? De Botton's work, as we see, follows a classic narrative design, even as it calls into question conventional understandings of narrative and employs a variety of modes to talk about and reflect on travel in contemporary culture.

Let us look more closely at the design of the work as a whole and in particular at the arrangement of events and their narration in the first section, 'On Anticipation', which falls under the first major heading, DEPARTURE. *The Art of Travel* is organized under five major headings or chapters: DEPARTURE; MOTIVES; LANDSCAPE; ART; RETURN. These serve to provide a kind of architecture for the book, lending it a partly temporal, partly structural and thematic movement. From the beginning (DEPARTURE) to the end of a journey/set of journeys (RETURN) via exploration of the purposes of and motivations for travel (MOTIVES), both personal and societal, the book treats nature (LANDSCAPE) and culture (ART) as stimuli for travel as well as mediators of it. DEPARTURE itself is subdivided into two sections, the first 'On Anticipation' and the second 'On Travelling Places'. Each deals with aspects of the decision to travel, the first focusing on preparations in advance of travel, the pleasures of anticipation and the gap between imagination and reality in terms of actual experience of a place. The second turns to the mechanics of travel and is concerned with the how, rather than the why of travel, focusing on the portals and liminal spaces through which we move on our journeys by train, aeroplane or car.

Section 1, On Anticipation, is itself divided into eight numbered subsections of varying lengths. These blocks of text with different but interrelated lines of narrative serve to create polyphony insofar as there are leitmotifs which recur at intervals in the narrative. A summary of the content of the different subsections will help to show how this interleaving of different textual blocks takes place.

Subsection 1: Description of the climatic conditions and their effect on the narrator, leading to his present disposition: a certain vulnerability and impressionability upon the arrival on his doorstep of a 'Winter Sun' brochure, a state which leads to his resolution to travel to the island of Barbados.

Subsection 2: A short interrogation of the place of travel in our pursuit of happiness and a critique of the lack of philosophical work dealing with the whys and wherefores of travel as opposed to information about destinations and how best to reach them.

Subsection 3: Inquiry into the relationship between anticipation and the reality of travel via introduction of a summary of the themes of J-K Huysmann's novel *A Rebours*, published in 1884, in which the hero, the Duc des Esseintes, finds greater pleasure in imagining places and experiencing them virtually than in actually seeing them. This subsection thematizes the potential gap between image or imagination and actual experience.

Subsection 4: Framed by the foregoing discussion re the delights of anticipation, the narrator reveals his own ideas about Barbados prior to visiting the island and compares his images in imagination to the reality of what he finds. He concludes that the skeletal nature of his imaginings, that is, the fact that he could focus at will only on certain aspects of what he expected to find, contributed to his pleasure. In actuality, he was bombarded by so many different sense impressions that it was difficult to take it all in. He goes on to hypothesize that it is this very process of selection and simplification in art and in imagination which contributes to the pleasure one feels. He sees memory as working in a similar way.

Subsection 5: Another short subsection picking up the story of Des Esseintes in relation to a journey made to Holland and Des Esseintes' subsequent realization that he felt more in tune with Holland and all things Dutch by looking at selected images in a museum than actually being there.

Subsection 6: Returning to his experiences on the island of Barbados, the narrator tries to reconstitute his movements and thoughts on that first morning and realizes that his efforts at description fail to render the details of his experience. He points to the fact that well-ordered paragraphs do not truly reflect the movements of actual consciousness and the confusions and fluctuations of lived experience. He goes on to muse on the fact that he cannot escape from himself just by moving from one location to another and acknowledges that perhaps it is easier to forget oneself by reading about and seeing images of other places than in actually being elsewhere. In anticipation and in memory, he concludes, things have a purity which they may not have in actuality.

Subsection 7: The narrator continues his relation of aspects of his stay on Barbados, recounting a trip he and his companion made round the island and a lunch that ended in an argument. This leads him to reflect on the key ingredients of happiness which are not always material or aesthetic but relate to a sense of psychological well-being.

Subsection 8: The final subsection returns to Des Esseintes and his decision to travel no more save in imagination. The narrator indicates that while he has continued to travel, he has some sympathy with Des Esseintes' position and has experienced as much, if not more, pleasure in anticipation than in actuality.

In outlining the content of the subsections which make up section 1 of DEPARTURE, my aim has been to highlight the way in which the lines of narrative intersect and converge and to point to the principal themes of the book. There are essentially two parallel stories here: that of de Botton and his trip to Barbados (subsections 1, 4, 6, 7) and that of Des Esseintes and his various trips, both actual and those made in imagination (subsections 3, 5, 8). The thoughts and insights of the fictional nineteenth-century traveller guide and underpin de Botton's own views of and reactions to travel. In addition, de Botton makes clear the influence of images, as well as descriptions of places, on his, and indeed fellow-travellers' dispositions and asks questions about our motivations for travel. In the course of 'On Anticipation' not only do the lines of narrative interpenetrate and converge but the meditations on travel that are originally separated out (cf. subsection 2, for example) begin to merge and feed into the remaining subsections.

Examination of the structure and thematic content of the first section has, hopefully, served to show how the section functions in terms of narrative progression, that is, taking the story forward as well as in terms of the organization of themes and motifs (e.g. the pleasures of anticipation vs. the potential disappointments of actuality; imagination vs. reality). It should also have made clear the musical counterpoint at work within the section. Bearing in mind discussion of novels such as Virginia Woolf's *The Waves*, which, it was argued, create coherence at the level of themes and motifs, rather than necessarily at the level of story or plot, we can see that this kind of coherence is also typical of de Botton's work. The preference for shortish blocks of text within a section creates a disruption of narrative progression at the level of story while at the same time carrying it forward at a different narrative level, that of the development of themes and motifs.

However, it is not only across subsections but also within some subsections that there appears to be a mixing and blending of apparently different modes of writing such as exposition, narrative, description, philosophical meditation. There are a number of points to be made here. Even prototypical narrative texts, such as nineteenth-century novels, can be seen to be composed of a mix of narrative, description and commentary. *Great Expectations*, for example, while telling the story of Pip's social transformation from blacksmith's apprentice to young gentleman in receipt of a fortune and the eventual disclosure of the true source of his money, uses a variety of means to move the story forward and fill in details of the social landscape and motivations of the characters. Within this, both description and commentary have a role to play, the latter often a consequence of the mature Pip's evaluation of the conduct of his younger self. Likewise, in *The Art of Travel*, the different discourses are in the service of progressing a story and inquiry into why we travel from the perspective of a living character whose perceptions are mediated by the views of other writers and artists from the past.

This mixing and blending is already apparent in the first subsection leading up to de Botton's decision to travel to Barbados. The opening sentences trade off what could be 'fictional', rather than 'factual', status, beginning like a Realist novel. 'It was hard to say when exactly winter arrived. The decline was gradual, like that of a person into old age, inconspicuous from day to day until the season became an established relentless reality' (de Botton, 2003, p. 5). In trying to pin down the novelistic elements here, we might point to the use of a simile, comparing the encroaching winter to the aging process in humans. The opening also seems to begin in medias res, as in a novel. It is not until the end of the subsection that the reader understands the motivation for what seems to be pure description and realizes that the weather together with the arrival of a 'Winter Sun' brochure conspire to resolve the author-narrator to travel to a sunnier clime in search of an antidote to his increasingly depressive mood.

The first paragraph goes on to outline more precisely the changing patterns of weather before once again resorting to another comparison, this time from the world of art history.

> By December, the new season was entrenched and the city was covered almost every day by an ominous steely-grey sky, like one in a painting by Mantegna or Veronese, the perfect backdrop to the crucifixion of Christ or to a day beneath the bedclothes. (de Botton, 2003, p. 5)

The comparison is not arbitrary in that it serves not only to reinforce the 'picture' being presented of a grey and not very inspiring day but also to introduce the idea of mediation of our vision of the world through art, an idea that will be further examined in the course of the book.

These descriptions of the rather miserable weather serve to create the backdrop against which to set the actions of the rather vulnerable author-narrator. Passing a park near his home, during a downpour one evening, he recalls how:

> in the intense heat of the previous summer, I had stretched out on the ground and let my bare feet slip from my shoes to caress the grass and how this direct contact with the earth had brought with it a sense of freedom and expansiveness, summer breaking down the usual boundaries between indoors and out, and allowing me to feel as much at home in the world as in my own bedroom. (de Botton, 2003, p. 5)

As well as adding to the evidence of the seasonal change in climatic conditions and its influence upon the mood, the long, final sentence of the opening paragraph serves to tell the reader something about the author-narrator and the kind of person/a he is. Paragraph 2 of subsection 1 contrasts the park in summer with the park in winter and further explores the author-narrator's change in mood. Paragraph 3 introduces the arrival of the 'Winter Sun' brochure and represents de Botton's reaction to it. The description begins 'objectively' but then goes on to indicate the 'subjective' feelings of the author-narrator and to acknowledge that his reading of the photographs is influenced by other pictorial representations of the exotic.

> Its cover displayed a row of palm trees, many of them growing at an angle, on a sandy beach fringed by a turquoise sea, set against a backdrop of hills, where I imagined there to be waterfalls and relief from the heat in the shade of sweet-smelling fruit trees. The photographs reminded me of the paintings of Tahiti that William Hodges had brought back from his journey with Captain Cook, showing a tropical lagoon in soft evening light where smiling local girls cavorted carefree (and barefoot) through luxuriant foliage, images that had provoked wonder and longing when Hodges first exhibited them at the Royal Academy in the sharp winter of 1776 – and that continued to provide a model for subsequent depictions of tropical idylls, including the pages of 'Winter Sun'. (de Botton, 2003, p. 8)

There are a number of things to note here: de Botton acknowledges the power of the photograph in the brochure to trigger a certain reaction, a reaction primed by past pictorial representations of the 'exotic', as seen through Western eyes. The mediating role of the image in culture and its ability to affect the emotional and psychological state of the viewer is foregrounded here. What is also of interest is the fact that both 'high' and 'low' culture is portrayed as equally capable of achieving such effects. Indeed, from de Botton's perspective, a line can be drawn from the paintings of William Hodges to the generic photographs in the 'Winter Sun' brochure.

Both Tahiti Revisited, 1776 (de Botton, 2003, pp. 6–7) and a rather generic photo of a Barbados beach (p. 21) are reproduced in the course of 'On Anticipation'. Their inclusion in relation to de Botton's description and commentary serves to demonstrate the thematic and pictorial connection between them and to illustrate de Botton's point about the impact of the visual on our desires and imagination. As pictorial representations of the exotic, we read them in relation to one another and understand them to be fulfilling the same function across time and across media.

The penultimate paragraph of subsection 1 continues reflection on the power of images to induce a longing to travel, even where the forces of reason militate against it (e.g. lack of money). Exposure to these images of elsewhere and the implied contrast with the here and now is sufficient to lead to a statement of resolve by the end of the subsection: 'to travel to the island of Barbados' (p. 8).

What I have tried to do is to indicate how de Botton's work is consciously structured in terms of a minimal definition of narrative, which requires that a human or human-like protagonist undergo a change in state over time and that there be some apparent motivation for that change. More importantly, however, de Botton's work can be seen to constitute a narrative of supermodernity in the sense that it relates to and focuses on movement through liminal spaces and embodies reflection on non-places. It contrasts the specificity and limitations of place (e.g. the author's bedroom) with the construction of spaces of the imagination and demonstrates the reliance of individual perception and experience on social and cultural mediation.

In terms of narrative development, its artful combination of different discourses (expository, narrative, philosophical) and focus on 'the themes that haunt the contemporary era (advertising, image, leisure, freedom, travel)' (Augé, 2008, p. 67) as well as its method of creating blocks of text, which both intersect with and help to constitute lines of narrative, reflect a preference for the spatial, rather than the temporal, and demonstrate an interest in border crossing. In *The Art of Travel* we can see to what extent the concept of narrative has expanded as a result of having travelled across disciplinary and generic borders and evaluate the extent to which it has helped create new conditions of possibility for the art of narrative.

Ben Okri's *In Arcadia*

According to Fox (2005), Ben Okri's *In Arcadia* (2002) has been misunderstood by the many critics and commentators who felt the novel to be poor in comparison with Okri's earlier work, particularly his prize-winning novel, *The Famished Road* (1992). Fox argues that one of the reasons for this is the fact that *In Arcadia* is a work full of intertextual references and one which sees Okri grapple with the Western European literary tradition rather than continue to write in the mode he had developed in his earlier work that drew on a kind of African magic realism. Fox (2005, p. 2) characterizes *In Arcadia* as an 'extraordinarily innovative exercise in fictive philosophy' and goes on to look at the various genres and intertexts on which Okri draws in the construction of his work. For Fox, it is an 'aesthetic and signifying "hybridity" that gives the novel its very distinctive character' (p. 4) which he describes as a 'particularly complex amalgam of the European and African cultural traditions' (p. 5). He suggests that critics who might have come to see Okri as a particular kind of writer, for example as a postcolonial Nigerian writer, may have found *In Arcadia* more difficult to pigeonhole in respect of its interests and the scale of its ambition.

What is of interest in the present context of the travelling concept of narrative and narratives of travel is first Okri's articulation of a 'fictive philosophy' (p. 2) against the backdrop of the elaboration of a journey which is 'speculative and mythical as well as literal and real' (p. 5). Okri had in fact made a real-life journey from London to Arcadia in the Peloponnese to make a documentary film in the series 'Great Train Journeys' for the BBC in 1996 and to that extent it can be said that the journey in *In Arcadia* is based on 'the outer facts of a real journey as a vehicle for fictional characters' (Okri, 2002). Okri (2002) continues: 'The journey is real, but the people are invented.' In the book, a crew of seven, including Lao, the presenter, assembles at Waterloo Station to begin a journey in search of Arcadia that will take them from London via Paris to Switzerland and on to Greece. The novel begins with receipt of a message inviting the various crew members to attend a preparatory meeting for the proposed journey and finishes as the crew embark on the Swiss leg of their journey. While for some critics, this is further evidence of a work that simply runs out of steam, for Fox (2005, p. 13), it is rather that Okri has reached 'the climactic point towards which the metaphoric journey has been tending', and therefore a fitting ending, at the moment when a certain transformation in some of the characters seems to have taken place.

Such an assessment sits comfortably with a narrative account of the novel, since there is evidence of a change of state over time on the part of the main protagonist/s, in this case Lao, the narrator and presenter, and the film crew who accompany him. This transformation is made explicit and is discussed in the novel in what might be considered philosophical terms as the narrator brings into focus the gap between the outward 'facts' of the lives of the crew members, all of whom, in one way or another, are losers and no hopers, and their inner lives and aspirations. Conversations over dinner in a Paris restaurant, for example, indicate that some members of the crew, including Jim, the director, are in fact more self-aware and reflective than they appear and are in search of a better, more 'authentic', way of life, a way of life that they had forgotten or that was lost to them. The journey on which they embark, which revolves around a search for the Arcadian ideal or a kind of paradise on earth, seems, after a time, to work its magic on the crew and there are moments when they are visibly moved and transformed by the experience. These changes are first charted by and refracted through Lao, as narrator and central consciousness of the book, then by a third-person authorial narrator who focuses on the perceptions of Lao and his friend Mistletoe.

Second, there is the question of Okri's use of genre and intertextuality as critical and creative resource. As has already been mentioned, *In Arcadia* is a work that seems to have caused the critics problems in terms of generic classification. In her interview with the novelist, Judith Palmer (2002) asks 'why he felt the need to fix his meditations in the framework of a novel' and notes that in replying, the author 'bristles' before he continues:

I felt only fiction could examine all the inner dimensions and possibilities and create the right tensions [. . .]. It's like cooking something – in the first part I apply the heat, and then the pressure changes and the flavour begins to come out. (Palmer, 2002)

The question arises then of whether *In Arcadia* is 'fictive philosophy' (Fox, 2005), 'a sloppy, poorly written novel' (Ball, 2002), one that 'peters out' (Hickling, 2002) or a conscious attempt to blend philosophical meditations and the quest novel, using the journey as a kind of peg on which to hang questions of fundamental import to the novelist, such as the question of the real: 'Fiction, painting, music all the great forms are trying to get us to that place of true enchantment – the true reality – and once we touch that place, we are soothed, and we can cope' (Palmer, 2002).

For Okri, the role of art is to offer access to a higher reality, one which is often at odds with the here and now and offers the possibility of a transformation of human experience. *In Arcadia* can be said to explore the role of art in human existence, what it signifies, and why we appear to need it and want to hold on to it. As the third-person authorial narrator indicates, 'art is a dream of perfection. And the dream is always many realms away from the reality' (Okri, 2002, p. 165). In this sense, Okri's work is as much concerned with the spiritual and transcendant, as with the material and visible. As such, he is working against a strictly Realist tradition in novelistic terms. In combining philosophical meditations with narrative exposition, he is seeking to take the reader to a place of enchantment and a place of truth. 'The whole thing about this book', he tells Palmer (2002), 'is the desire to set sail from old selves, old assumptions, old negativities, old cramped reactions, towards being more free'. Just as the journey offers the crew the possibility of leaving behind their old selves and former lives, so *In Arcadia* offers Okri the opportunity to go beyond a particular idea of the novel and to create a work which represents a 'blending of earlier postcolonial attributes with some of the most persistent themes in the Western literary tradition' (Fox, 2005, p. 4)

Finally, there are parallels to be made with de Botton's modus operandi in *The Art of Travel.* Insofar as de Botton uses the tools of narrative to investigate what are essentially philosophical questions: why we travel and what it is we expect to find by travelling, there are clear points of contact with Okri's method in *In Arcadia.* For Okri employs the journey on which the crew embarks to explore the Arcadian ideal and what it has represented over the centuries. Their destination is to be Arcadia in the Peloponnese but en route they film people and places which bear some relation to aspects of the Arcadian ideal: the train driver who has transformed his suburban house into a little Arcadia by creating a beautiful English garden where there had been only stones and rubble; the false Arcadia of Versailles; and the painting by Poussin, *Les Bergers d'Arcadie* (The Arcadian Shepherds), described as 'the epitome and the finest realisation of the Arcadian notion in art' (Okri, 2002, p. 203). In addition, just as de Botton approaches place through the eyes of other artist-guides, so Okri's narrators (Lao and the authorial narrator), recount events and perceptions through a literary, philosophical and artistic prism. Indeed, as we shall see, the role of the visual and of vision is an important set of topoi in the novel.

Closer examination of the structural organization of the book helps to elucidate the way in which Okri has approached his topic. The work is divided into three Parts and seven Books, a division which is significant in terms of the novel's structural dynamic and thematic development. Part one consists of two books; Part two of three Books; and Part 3 of two Books. Each Book is further divided into numerical chapters or sections, some of them quite short, some rather longer, like passages from a musical composition. Part one deals with the preparations for the trip and the meeting of the crew at Waterloo; Part 2 relates the journey to Paris via the Channel Tunnel, their trip to the Parisian suburbs and the train driver's garden, their Parisian dinner and discussion of Arcadia and finally the trip to Versailles; Part three tells of their trip to the Louvre to see Poussin's painting, Les Bergers D'Arcadie (The Arcadian Shepherds) and their departure for Switzerland.

In terms of the design of the book there is a symmetry which reflects the dynamics of the classic three-act structure in film with set-up, confrontation and resolution (cf. Readman, 2003). Given that Okri originally presented a documentary film on Arcadia in which 'the novel follows the same path as the film' (Palmer, 2002), this is perhaps less surprising than it might otherwise appear. What is also of interest in the book is the focus on both place and space. For *In Arcadia* is a novel concerned with transit and border crossing as much as it is with recovery of place and lost ideals. The train journey from London to Paris is not simply an event but a passage away from the trials and tribulations of the crew's past lives towards their projected future selves. They register the landscape as the train speeds past only as a series of snapshots (Augé, 2008, p. 69), constructing, as they go, 'a fictional relationship between gaze and landscape' (pp. 69–70).

Indeed, discussions of the visual, of how what we see is often a projection or reflection of what has been made manifest in film, in painting and in imagination, is part of the thematic substance of the book. Lao is rather wary of what he considers to be the lies told by the camera which 'feeds on living flesh' (Okri, 2002, p. 21); he regards paintings as living things 'which carry on their normal busy comic or tragic transactions away from human gaze' (p. 200) and only freeze when humans look at them. He sees the world as 'a sprung text that we endlessly learn how to read better' (p. 154). What we see is a function of who we are. 'All true seeing is a testament to the person who sees. You see what you are. You create what you are. You read into a painting, into the world, what you are' (Okri, 2002, p. 155). This suggests a reciprocal relationship between reader and the world, between vision and imagination.

Reading, as much as writing, is a challenging activity, as far as Okri is concerned. In interview with Judith Palmer (2002), he makes clear that he is writing for the effect that a book will have on readers not necessarily, as they read, but in the future. 'I deliberately write for the "after" because it's not about the book, it's about the spirit. Books develop an organic relationship with the air. They can give rise to things you would never connect them with' (Palmer, 2002). Likewise, he is clear that as a writer, he is in the service of the reader and that while for him, writing is a kind of Arcadia, 'it's not the act of writing – it's what writing can yield up' (Palmer, 2002).

It is this sense of mission alongside a belief in the power of the invisible and the intangible to direct our lives that is characteristic of *In Arcadia*. The rather cynical and world-weary crew appears transformed as a result of their journey. While there are evil spirits which appear to hover over their journey (cf. Malasso), there is also the redemptive power of art and of nature. The modern world is characterized as an inferno (Okri, 2002, p. 5) and a place from which the crew is only too glad to escape. It is this metaphysical quest, a search for lost ideals that is the real driving force of the book. Okri's implied critique of modern living is reflected in the change which takes place in the crew, in particular Lao, as well as in the organization of the novel which comprises lyrical and philosophical sections or what may appear to be digressions in addition to the more conventional stretches of narrative.

For example, Part one, Book two contains four sections entitled 'Intuitions in the Garden', which treat Creation Myths and the Loss of an Earthly Paradise. Part two, Book three incorporates five sections entitled 'Intuitions in the Dark', a series of meditations on Death, sparked by travel through tunnels and under the sea in the Channel Tunnel. In addition, towards the end of Part two, there are a number of 'Intuitions' by members of the crew following their visit to Versailles. These 'Intuitions' revolve around their consciousness of Versailles as a false Arcadia. Part three, Book six begins with three sections entitled 'Intuitions before Dreaming' in which the role of painting in human endeavour is discussed. At the end of Part three, there are also two sections entitled 'Intuitions on the Way', which relate Mistletoe's thoughts as they leave Paris by train and head towards Switzerland. She muses on the role of mortality in shaping human actions and behaviour.

In terms of driving the 'plot' forward, these passages serve to disrupt narrative progression. Yet, insofar as this is a novel about the power of 'intuition' in human life, they are not digressions but rather interrogations of what might be considered fundamental human questions: how to live in a world which seems to have lost its way, how to 'escape from the inferno, through purgatory, to a recovered "true" paradise that transcends the sordid and debased imperfections of the fallen world' (Fox, 2005, p. 3). The novel suggests that it is through literature, art and appreciation of nature that we can recover a more balanced and peaceful existence.

In this regard, there are parallels with de Botton's *The Art of Travel* in which the outward journey is a pretext for inner travel and a search for the roots of well-being and happiness. Okri's *In Arcadia* is also a metaphysical journey structured around an actual journey. As the crew leave Britain behind and cross the border into France, they are already on the threshold of self-discovery, a process which is set to continue as they journey on to Switzerland and eventually reach Arcadia.

Conclusion

The present chapter has sought to bring into alignment the micro- and macro-levels of discussion about narrative by discussing two works of interest in relation to questions of genre and generic classification as well as in the light of discussion of the temporal and spatial axes of narrative. In posing in different ways questions about the relation of the physical to the metaphysical worlds and the nature and meaning of the journey both outward and inward, they are both concerned with borders and territories and with pushing the limits of narrative inquiry.

In the final analysis, neither de Botton nor Okri are travel writers per se, though de Botton holds the distinction of having been appointed as Heathrow's Writer-in-Residence in the summer of 2009 producing a book about his experience entitled, *A Week at the Airport*. Yet for both the concept of travel and of border crossing is very important in their work. Neither is content to continue to produce works which replicate what has already been done or which conform to generic expectations. Rather, their output shows them to be risk-takers and innovators who use genre as resource in the production of works which travel across boundaries and create new mixes of fact and fiction, literature and philosophy, narrative and exposition.

It is perhaps not by chance that both de Botton and Okri favour generically hybrid forms, given their status as writers who have grown up with different cultural traditions and who therefore have the possibility of accessing a range of literary and artistic models. De Botton was Swiss-born and grew up speaking French and German before being sent to England to be educated. He studied history at Cambridge and philosophy at King's College, London before eventually turning to full-time writing. In interview with Norman Goldman (2002), he claimed to have always 'had a taste for reflection on experience' and to have been 'particularly influenced by Proust, Montaigne, Stendhal and Flaubert at an impressionable age'.

Likewise Okri's ability to combine different genres in new ways and to add to the debate about and conceptualizations of Arcadianism (Fox, 2005, p. 15) depends on his location as a writer familiar with both Western and African traditions. What Fox sees as 'a distinctively postmodern rewriting of Utopia' (p. 15) and therefore the source of Okri's 'originality' must be understood in relation to Okri's crossing of generic and other boundaries. Indeed, in the context of a recent BBC World Service programme (19 July 2009), Okri speaks of the dependence of innovation in art and society on freedom, the freedom to depart from tradition and do something else, something otherwise. For Okri

(2009), 'our reality is richer than Realism implies'; at times it is important to move away from what we think we know and try something new. This is precisely what Okri continues to do in his work, even inventing a new form, the stoku, a blending of short story and the spirit of the haiku form, in his latest work, *Tales of Freedom* (2009).

This chapter has been concerned with narrative's relation to travel across a number of dimensions, both literal and metaphoric. Journeys can of course be physical, a displacement from A to B, but they can also, simultaneously, be psychological and metaphysical, as we saw in relation to de Botton's *The Art of Travel* and Okri's *In Arcadia*. Yet travel is not just concerned with mobility and movement but also with relations between people and places, with visual perception and cultural and textual mediation, and with the construction of the near and the elsewhere. It is about space as well as place and is concerned with the impact on individual consciousness of experience of cultural contact.

Indeed, there appears to be a confluence of attendant and interrelated issues around narrative which are being 'played out' in relation to narratives of travel. By this, I mean to point not simply to increasing interest in the travelogue and narratives of travel evidenced across fields such as Cultural Studies, Postcolonial Studies and Gender Studies (Korte, 2008) but also to the role of the journey in all its dimensions as a structuring principle of narrative itself. The grand narratives of colonization and imperialism are increasingly being challenged by the narrative accounts of the colonized and previously marginalized individuals and/or groups are finding a voice. As Korte (2008, p. 620) indicates regarding what she calls the area of 'cultural narratology', travelogues and travel fiction are being analysed 'for their projection of culture-specific discourses (e.g. orientalist or imperialist), their constructions of alterity and self-identities, their imagings of countries and peoples, or as phenomena of inter-culturality'.

At the same time, narrative representations of histories, whether based on actuality or imagined, and the stories of individuals and social groups are no longer the prerogative of Western, usually male, writers. Chimamanda Ngozi Adichie, author of *Half of a Yellow Sun*, published in 2006, is an example of the new generation of writers of fiction whose narratives weave together the public and private, politics and history, using particular narrative structures and features (e.g. embedded narratives; different lines of narrative and multiple perspectives) to critique and, in a sense, rewrite dominant histories, in her case the causes and outcomes of the Biafran War and the establishment of Nigerian Independence.

The case studies addressed in this chapter were chosen to pick up on aspects of an ongoing, multifaceted debate, differently focused depending on disciplinary area but nevertheless relating to a cluster of issues around travel and writing; cultural translation and mediation; generic transformation and notions of hybridity. These questions relate to narrative both directly and indirectly: directly in relation to the issue of what constitutes or counts as a narrative, what the prototypical features of particular types of narrative might be, and where narrative appears to be headed. At a broader, metaphoric and translational level, they echo some of the key themes in narrative studies today in its concern with the politics of cultural transfer, with questions of narrative voice, and with how narratives are constituted, disseminated, received and adapted across cultures, as well as across modes and media, in other words, how they travel, both temporally and spatially/geographically.

Chapter 7

Contemporary Narratives:
Concluding Remarks

This book has been concerned primarily with the state of narrative affairs today and with identifying key trends and issues in contemporary narrative production. It has taken the view that there are a number of factors and forces of particular relevance in understanding the shape and substance of narratives in the twenty-first century and that these may be seen to relate, broadly speaking, to the area of multimodality and multiliteracies. In respect of multimodality, the emphasis has been on a move away from the primacy of the verbal towards an interest in exploring the impact of other modalities on verbal or written communication, most notably, though not exclusively, the influence of the visual. In respect of multiliteracies, the premise has been that writers who are able to draw on more than one set of representational resources in constructing their narratives are at an advantage in terms of creative potential. While such a position is not uncontroversial, analysis of novels such as *Brick Lane* and *Dictionary for Lovers* has served to point to the ways in which diversity of linguistic cultures and notions of cultural translation can underwrite narrative production.

The first point, increased interest in the visual has a number of dimensions: while it includes works which incorporate visual elements into the design and elaboration of the narrative (e.g. Guo's *UFO in Her Eyes*) or which have parallel and interacting visual and verbal narratives (e.g. Sebald's *Austerlitz*), it would also include works triggered by a visual source – we might think here of Tracy Chevalier's *Girl with a Pearl Earring*. As recently as 16 March 2010, an article in *The Guardian* pointed to a collaboration between the National Portrait Gallery and a number of writers, such as John Banville, Joanna Trollope and Tracy Chevalier, who were given the opportunity to imagine the lives of the anonymous subjects whose portraits had been painted in the sixteenth- and seventeenth centuries and lain hidden in a storeroom in the gallery. Their short fictions, written in response to a particular portrait, were based on their animation of (aspects of) the lives of their chosen subjects using the printed word. For, as Mitchell (2002) reminds us, one of the perhaps unforeseen, unintended consequences of a contemporary focus on visual culture has been the failure to notice that literature is essentially a mixed medium. He speaks of 'the stunning redundancy of declaring literature to be a verbal and not a visual medium'

(p. 174) and points to 'techniques like ekphrasis and description, as well as [. . .] more subtle strategies of formal arrangement' which involve 'virtual or imaginative experiences of space and vision that are no less real for being indirectly conveyed through language' (p. 174). Such a sentiment echoes Kress's contention that all texts, including the seemingly purely verbal, have multimodal potential (Kress, 2003) and reflects the increased interest among narrative theorists and analysts in concepts of space, whether this be the mental space of the storyworld constructed by the reader on the basis of textual cues provided by the writer or aspects of the layout and sequencing which are likely to impact upon its reception (see, for example, Herman, 2002).

In relation to the second point, the concept of multiliteracies refers to access to multiple literacies, which includes digital literacy and the ability to create online narratives (such as that produced by the makers of *Inanimate Alice*, Kate Pullinger and Chris Joseph) as well as the ability to use different linguistic and representational systems in the making of a piece of fiction. It is perhaps not by chance that Barbara Kingsolver, the recent winner of the Orange Prize for Fiction, whose novel, *The Lacuna*, moves between the US and Mexico and draws on characters both factual and fictional, is a speaker of Spanish as well as English and has lived and worked in a variety of locations in many parts of the world including in Africa, the Canaries, France and South America. The underlying point is that it is access to resources, be they linguistic, cultural, technological and/or social, that enables writers to experiment and take risks. As we have seen, following Bhabha (1994), newness enters the world through processes of translation and transformation and as a consequence of the creation of a third space where otherwise heterogeneous and diverse elements can co-exist. This third or hybrid space is not just a product of access to different cultures, different languages or different literacy practices but relates also to ways of combining and mixing different genres (e.g. the dictionary-novel). As we have seen, narrative itself can be seen as a genre (e.g. narrative text as opposed to argumentative or persuasive text) or as a mode which can be combined with other modes in interesting and eclectic ways. Insofar as narrative relates to the construction of a story and involves a character or characters whose situation changes over time, there is no fixed form for narrative, though there are sets of conventions that accrue around narratives at particular historical periods and in particular disciplinary areas (cf. what is seen to constitute a media narrative or a film narrative). Yet in order for new types and forms of narrative to emerge, these conventions are often contravened (cf. Woolf's rejection of the conventions of what at that time was seen to constitute a certain kind of realism in the novel). The question then arises of what is deemed to be the best and most apt means at any given time for representing or translating aspects of reality, on the assumption that the stories we tell bear some relation to the world around us and of our perceived place in them. My purpose here has not been to examine the reasons for human storytelling but rather to consider the factors shaping their narrative production today.

If the metaphor of translation has been used throughout the book to gather together the various strands explored, it is because it permits connections to be made between different aspects of narrative development. For example, a move from visual to verbal, such as that undertaken by the writers collaborating on the National Portrait Gallery project, can be seen as a kind of translation insofar as the canvas represents an existing source text on which the writer is able to draw in the construction of a new target text consisting of an imagined storyline. While the degree of constraint is likely to be variable, the writer is nevertheless required to cast light upon the otherwise anonymous subjects by creating a life history for them or imagining a segment of that life on the basis of what they see or imagine themselves to see, since vision too is mediated by knowledge and by culture, as well as being a response to sensory impressions. Artistic vision in this instance becomes the ability to translate into words a slice of life captured on canvas or to turn a static image into a more dynamic verbal composition.

Translation has also been helpful in representing the process by which images, ideas, and indeed narratives, move across borders, requiring re-presentation and re-interpretation by individuals and groups with the requisite expertise and interest. Increased migration and mobility, whether voluntary or enforced, create the conditions for translation in both a broad and a narrow sense. As Apter (2006) has pointed out, post-9/11 issues of conflict resolution and the ability to communicate across cultures have become increasingly important. Whether it be across nations or within nations, these zones of contact between and among people with different languages and cultures open up the possibility of co-existence and interaction. From such interaction, new cultural and artistic configurations can emerge. Just as many writers engage in translation as a means of regenerating their own work and/or learning from, as well as disseminating, the work of others (e.g. Proust's translations of Ruskin), so those who cross borders or live in zones of cultural contact have the possibility of importing new material and methods into their work.

Venuti (1993) reminds us of the violence effected by translation and of the need for an ethics of translation in a world where English continues to exercise cultural hegemony and where the volume of literature translated into English from other languages is far less than that translated out of English (Venuti, 1993, p. 210). While my rather broad conception of translation might appear to factor out the political and be seen as rather cavalier, it in fact recognizes the inequalities, while wishing to turn them on their head in two main respects: first, insofar as my argument has been that access to representational resources is a condition of creative narrative production, it privileges bilingual, bicultural and multilingual, multicultural writers, as well as those who cross borders, both literally and metaphorically. Second, it is sensitive to Venuti's notion of foreignization as an appropriate translation strategy for writers and translators today. Indeed, what I have tried to suggest with respect to the construction of Hasina's letters in *Brick Lane* is precisely that Ali (2004) can be seen as having adopted such a translation strategy. I have also indicated, in relation to Guo (2007), that use of Chinese English or English accented in a Chinese way is a strategy of resistance to the imposition of a particular variety of English. While the dominance and seeming ubiquity of English can be seen to pose a threat to other languages, it can also be argued that as a historical and material resource, English as a lingua franca has the potential to construct a creative and productive linguistic space where it can be used flexibly and in accordance with the motivations and purposes of the particular writer regardless of place or places of origin. The corollary of this trend in creating new varieties of English would be the rise of the regional novel or the novel written in dialect such that the distinctiveness of a character's or narrator's voice is heard. The controversial winner of the 1994 Booker Prize, James Kelman, is an example of a writer keenly aware of what it means to write using the rhythms and cadences as well as the syntax and lexis of regional varieties of English in the face of dominant English norms and expectations. His Glaswegian-inflected English can be seen as a politically, as well as artistically, motivated choice.

Another characteristic of *Contemporary Narrative* has been a focus on what it means to tell stories across modes and media and what is involved in the process of adaptation. Discussion of such processes from the perspective of practitioners who also reflect on and write about their own practice (e.g. Minghella, Mitchell) has shown the extent to which there is recognition of the specificities of a particular mode or medium (cf. Minghella's example of sentence grammar vs. film grammar and the difference between 'telling' and 'showing') at the same time as there is a determination to rise to the challenge of transposing a storyline and/or what is deemed essential about a narrative from one medium to another. Rather like debates in Translation Studies regarding notions of equivalence and/or fidelity, there are different takes on the extent to which this is possible or desirable. Minghella's cinematographic *The Talented Mr. Ripley* is not the same as Highsmith's novel. Indeed, Minghella points to conscious changes to Highsmith's novel to accommodate the different affordances of the medium. Yet the two bear a strong resemblance to one another and the contours of the story have been preserved even as the focus has changed. Minghella articulates his concern as having been with motivation and with a kind of psycho-geography created as a consequence of his aim to demonstrate psychological motivation on Ripley's part and in the light of the cinematographic constraints under which he was operating. Mitchell also seemed concerned to 'translate' aspects of what she had always admired about Woolf's prose – its visual quality and poetic rhythms – into a multimedia spectacle which tried to capture both the iterability and change (repetition with difference) of Woolf's novel, while drawing attention to the consciously crafted nature of the theatrical experience. Some of the qualities and concerns of Woolf's fiction – its focus on the ephemeral nature of experience, for example; its interest in luminosity and in change and transformation over time – were captured, if only fleetingly, in the staging and lighting of the production and in the degree to which it embodied the competing demands of scripted and sequenced events and improvised action.

While the focus of the book has been a conscious attempt to identify the traits and concerns of a selection of narratives and address the question of possible new directions in contemporary narrative, the book has also drawn out and drawn on what might be termed a theory of creativity. Both the metaphor of translation and notions of cultural transformation have emphasized the potential of prior or pre-existing works in offering writers a source text for creative transposition or re-creation. The examples of Winterson and Ali Smith have served to demonstrate the sometimes self-conscious but nonetheless deliberate manner in which writers treat what Winterson refers to as strong texts (Winterson, 1995). Clearly, writers absorb all sorts of ideas, images and information from various sources which may or may not be reflected in their books and/or traced back to a source. My purpose here is not to denigrate the creativity of writers but to present that creativity as a product of interaction and responsiveness to other texts and other writers rather than as a mark of genius or originality inherent in the person of the writer. In examining the construction of narratives today and exposing the forces which serve to shape them (access to certain types of knowledge; representational, cultural and technological resources), I have indicated the writer's dependence on and debt to a pre-existing narrative tradition. Whether or not they consciously acknowledge their reliance on and transformation of such a tradition or literary lineage, as do Winterson and Smith, for example, is not in question. What is at issue is rather the manifold ways in which the 'writer is an instrument of transformation' (Winterson, 1995, p. 25), translating the lines and uncovering the folds of the old to create a new (imagined and imaginational) space.

Glossary of Key Terms and Concepts

ADAPTATION

This refers to the process by which works originally produced in a particular medium are reworked and modified in order to be suitable for production in a different medium. For example, novels are often adapted into screenplays and are subsequently turned into films.

ANALEPSIS

This term refers to an ordering of events in the story such that the reader is transported back to a point in the past. It is the equivalent of flashback in film.

CULTURAL TRANSLATION

This is a term originating in Social Anthropology which has been picked up by theorists in Postcolonial Studies and Translation Studies. Originally it referred to the work done by social anthropologists seeking to represent the culture of other, usually distant, peoples for a relatively homogeneous audience at home. Today, its application is wider: while it may still refer to the process of representing and explicating another culture or cultures, it may also refer to the condition of migrancy in general, that is people transported from one culture to another – and to the situation of many postcolonial subjects in particular who are the products of more than one language and culture.

DISCOURSE	In relation to narrative, discourse refers to the language chosen to relate the story.
DOMESTICATION	Where a translator aims at eliminating in his/her work, through his/her choice of language, all signs that this is a work in translation and tries to present it as if it were originally written in the target language, we can speak of domestication.
ENGLISH AS A LINGUA FRANCA (ELF)	This refers to an evolving view of English as it is used today, mainly but not exclusively, by speakers of other languages for purposes of communication and expression. It points to the ways in which communication is effected in international contexts by users whose goal is to get their meaning across using all the resources at their disposal.
FOREIGNIZATION	Where a translator emphasizes the difference in languages and cultural systems through his/her use of a translation strategy aimed at confronting the reader with the fact that they are reading a work in translation, we can speak of foreignization.
FUNCTIONAL SPECIALIZATION	This refers to the specific attributes and affordances of particular modes and to the fact that some modes may be better than others for realizing specific purposes.
GENRE	The term genre relates to groups of text which are seen to share particular structural and thematic properties or which consist of common modes of organization or rhetorical moves. While genres are relatively stable entities, they

may evolve over time or disappear altogether as new genres come into being. The distribution and subsistence of genres is a social phenomenon.

HETERODIEGETIC NARRATOR

This refers to a narrator who is not a protagonist in the story which s/he tells.

HOMODIEGETIC NARRATOR

This refers to a narrator who is also a protagonist in the story which s/he is telling.

HYBRIDITY

In the context of the irreducibility of cultural and linguistic difference, hybridity was a term used by Bhabha to refer to the creation of a third space which was the product of a particular mix.

INTERCULTURAL TRANSLATION

This refers to the consequence of a process of moving across and between languages and cultures, each of which is rooted in a different set of behaviours and conventions.

INTERLANGUAGE

In Second Language Acquisition, the term interlanguage is used to refer to the language produced by a learner as s/he negotiates the process of moving from a first language (L1) towards ('mastery' of) a second language (L2). I use the term not to suggest a deficit model of language learning but to point to the possibilities inherent in combining two or more languages.

INTERMEDIAL TRANSLATION

This refers to the process by which a text is re-presented in a different medium. This would include what happens when a story originally produced in print form is adapted for the stage or the screen.

INTERMODAL TRANSLATION

This term describes the process whereby a set of signs in one mode is transferred to or translated into another (e.g. a move from visual to verbal).

INTERTEXTUALITY

This is based on a theory of text which believes that there is dialogue between and among texts and that the fabric of new works is woven from pre-existing words and stretches of discourse formed into new combinations. Often references from and allusions to previous texts can be found in the work of contemporary writers.

MEDIUM

This refers to the physical base which carries or channel which transmits a message. Written text, for example, can be printed in a magazine, newspaper or book or it can appear on a computer screen and be transmitted via electronic means.

MISE EN ABYME

This refers to a literary technique whereby a tale, embedded in the story being told, may parallel the features and contours of the main story or may connect with or relate to it in some way.

MODE

Mode refers to the different ways in which text can be realized. It may consist, for example, of words and images, thereby incorporating the visual and verbal modes.

MOTIVATED SIGN

This refers to a motivated, rather than arbitrary, conjunction of signifier and signified.

MULTIMODALITY

This term encompasses a view of text which emphasizes the way in which different modes (e.g. the verbal and the visual) combine to make meaning.

NARRATIVE

The term narrative is used to refer to a tale told by a narrator. The

NARRATOLOGY

tale may involve the narrator him/herself or may involve a representation of the actions and thoughts of others.

This refers to the science of narrative, a structuralist attempt to develop a rigorous and systematic approach to the study of narrative, with a view to identifying its essential properties or elements and trying to create a typology of narrative.

NARRATOR

A narrator is the person or persons responsible for telling a particular story. S/he may relate his/her own story or that of someone else.

PROLEPSIS

This refers to the narration of events such that there is mention of something which is yet to happen, from the perspective of chronological sequence. It is equivalent to the flashforward in film.

READING PATH

Reading path is a term which points to the ways in which different texts suggest, if not require, different modes of apprehension and negotiation, as the reader or viewer attempts to navigate through them. Reading paths may also be culturally prescribed (cf. reading English vs. reading Chinese or Arabic).

SPATIALIZATION

Spatialization refers to the manner in which the linear quality of narratives is challenged by a disruption of sequence, through, for example, the intercalation of images and/or a focus on the spatial qualities of the narrative.

STORY

The term story refers to the sequence of events which make up the narrative.

STORY ORDER

This term refers to the chronological arrangement of the elements of a story.

STORYWORLD

This refers to the virtual world to which readers relocate as they construct a mental model of the universe represented in the narrative.

SOURCE TEXT

This is a term used in Translation Studies to refer to an originary text or the text to be translated from one language into another.

TARGET TEXT

This refers to the text produced as a result of a process of translation from a source text.

TEMPORALIZATION

Temporalization refers to the devices used to emphasize the temporal dimension of a narrative and/or to present images in relation to the changes effected on them by the passage of time.

TEXT

A narrow definition of text would see it as a coherent stretch of spoken or written discourse which is constructed in such a way that it can stand alone. A broader view would include cultural as well as linguistic artefacts, constructed to convey information and express ideas as well as communicate a set of values.

TEXT ORDER

This relates to the order in which events are narrated and may contrast with story order.

TRANSFORMATION

This term relates to a process of text production resulting from dialogue and interaction with prior texts. It places value on the inherent creativity of language and sees writing in terms of a series of modifications of pre-existing texts.

TRANSLATION

In a narrow sense, translation refers to the transfer of information and ideas originally conveyed in one language into another language or languages. In a broader sense, translation can be seen to refer to the transfer of information and ideas which appear to be rooted in a particular environment (whether this be linguistic, social and/or cultural) in a way which demonstrates awareness of difference.

References

Ali, M. (2004), *Brick Lane*. London: Black Swan.
—(2006), *Alentejo Blue*. London: Doubleday.
—(2009), *In the Kitchen*. London: Doubleday.
Apter, E. (2006), *The Translation Zone: A New Comparative Literature*. Princeton, NJ and Oxford: Princeton University Press.
Asad, T. (1986), 'The concept of cultural translation in British social anthropology', in J. Clifford and G. Marcus (eds), *Writing Culture: The Poetics and Politics of Ethnography*. Berkeley, Los Angeles, CA and London: University of California, pp. 141–64.
Augé, M. (2008), *Non-Places: An Introduction to Supermodernity*. London and New York: Verso.
Bakhtin, M. (2004), 'Forms of time and chronotope in the novel', in M. Holquist (ed.), *The Dialogic Imagination: Four Essays by M. M. Bakhtin*. Austin, TX: University of Texas Press, pp. 84–258.
Bal, M. (1997), *Narratology: Introduction to the Theory of Narrative* (second edn). Toronto, Buffalo, NY and London: University of Toronto Press.
Ball, M. (2002), 'A review of *In Arcadia* by Ben Okri'. *The Compulsive Reader*. Available online at: http://www.compulsivereader.com/html/index.php?name=News&file=article&sid=367 (accessed 5 November 2010).
Barthes, R. (1970a), *Mythologies*. Paris: Editions du Seuil.
—(1970b), *S/Z*. Paris: Editions du Seuil.
—(1977), *Image, Music, Text*. London: Fontana Press.
Bassnett, S. (2002), *Translation Studies* (third edn). London: Routledge.
Bassnett, S. and P. Bush (eds) (2006), *The Translator as Writer*. London and New York: Continuum.
Bhabha, H. (1994), 'How newness enters the world', in H. Bhabha, *The Location of Culture*. London and New York: Routledge, pp. 303–37.
Bradbury, M. (1989), *The Modern World: Ten Great Writers*. London: Penguin Books.
Bricknell, T. (ed.) (2005), *Minghella on Minghella*. London: Faber and Faber.
Brooks, P. (2000), Extract from *Reading for the Plot*, in M. McQuillan (ed.), *The Narrative Reader*. London and New York: Routledge, pp. 145–52.
Cacciottolo, M. (2006), 'Brick Lane protesters hurt over "lies"'. *BBC News*, 31 July 2006. Available online at: http://news.bbc.co.uk/1/hi/5229872.stm (accessed 15 November 2010).
Campbell, C. (2007), 'Katie Mitchell on *Waves*'. Interview at the Cottesloe Theatre with Katie Mitchell, 12 January 2007. The podcast can be found at: http://www.nationaltheatre.org.uk/?lid=23945.
Cobley, P. (2001), *Narrative*. London and New York: Routledge.

Cormack, A. (2006), 'Migration and the politics of narrative form: realism and the postcolonial subject in Brick Lane'. *Contemporary Literature*, 47, (4), 695–721.

de Botton, A. (2003), *The Art of Travel*. London: Penguin Books.

—(2009), *A Week at the Airport: A Heathrow Diary*. London: Profile Books.

de Lauretis, T. (2000), 'Desire in narrative', in M. McQuillan (ed.), *The Narrative Reader*. London and New York: Routledge, pp. 204–12.

Derrida, J. (1981), 'The law of genre', in W. J. T. Mitchell (ed.), *On Narrative*. Chicago and London: University of Chicago Press.

Dickens, C. (1986), *Great Expectations*. Harmondsworth: Penguin Books.

Doloughan, F. (2005), 'Reading images, telling tales: meaning-making and the culture of narrativity'. *International Journal of Learning*, 11, 1697–1701. Common Ground Publishing Pty Ltd. at www. Learning-Journal.com.

—(2009), 'Bottling the imagination: writing as metamorphosis in Ali Smith's *Girl Meets Boy*'. Conference paper delivered at the International Creative Writing Conference, University of Bangor, 19–21 June 2009.

Dorfman, A. (1999), *Heading South, Looking North: A Bilingual Journey*. London: Penguin Books.

Durden, M. (2003), 'The poetics of absence: photography in the aftermath of war', in P. Seawright, *Hidden*. London: The Imperial War Museum.

Eco, U. (2003), *Mouse or Rat? Translation as Negotiation*. London: Weidenfeld and Nicolson.

Falk, E. (1981), *The Poetics of Roman Ingarden*. Chapel Hill, NC: The University of North Carolina Press.

Flint, K. (1992), 'Introduction', in V. Woolf, *The Waves*. London: Penguin Books, pp. ix–xl.

Fox, A. (2005), 'In search of the postmodern utopia: Ben Okri's *In Arcadia*'. *Portal Journal of Multidisciplinary International Studies*, 2, (2). Available online at: http://epress.lib.uts.edu.au/ojs/index.php/portal/article/viewArticle/115 (accessed 5 November 2010).

Gaiman, N. and D. McKean (2007), *Signal to Noise*. London: Bloomsbury Publishing.

Genette, G. (1983), *Narrative Discourse: An Essay in Method*. New York: Cornell University Press.

Gibson, A. (2000), Extract from *Towards a Postmodern Theory of Narrative*, in M. McQuillan (ed.), *The Narrative Reader*. London and New York: Routledge, pp. 152–7.

Goldman, N. (2002), 'Interview with Alain de Botton – author of *The Art of Travel*'. Available online at: http://www.bookpleasures.com/Lore2/idx/67/1184/General_NonFiction/article/Interview_With_Alain_de_BottonAuthor_of_The_Art_Of_Travel.html and http://www.writerspace.com/interviews/botton1002.html (accessed 15 November 2010).

Guillén, C. (1993), *The Challenge of Comparative Literature*. Translated by C. Franzen (1993). Cambridge, MA and London: Harvard University Press.

Guo, X. (2007), *A Concise Chinese-English Dictionary for Lovers*. London: Chatto and Windus.

—(2008), *20 Fragments of a Ravenous Youth*. London: Chatto and Windus.

—(2009), *UFO in Her Eyes*. London: Chatto and Windus.

—(2010), *Lovers in the Age of Indifference*. London: Chatto and Windus.

Harrell, D. and J. Zhu (2009), 'Agency play: dimensions of agency for interactive narrative design'. Symposium paper at the Association for the Advancement of Artificial Intelligence, Spring 2009, pp. 44–52. Available online at: http://www.aaai.org/Papers/Spring/2009/SS-09–06/SS09–06-008.pdf (accessed 15 November 2010).

Herman, D. (2002), *Story Logic: The Problems and Possibilities of Narrative.* Lincoln, NE: The University of Nebraska Press.

—(2007), 'Introduction', in D. Herman (ed.), *The Cambridge Companion to Narrative.* Cambridge and New York: Cambridge University Press, pp. 3–21.

—(2010), 'Word-image/utterance-gesture: case studies in multimodal storytelling', in R. Page (ed.), *New Perspectives on Narrative and Multimodality.* New York and Abingdon: Routledge, pp. 78–98.

Hickling, A. (2002), 'Tunnel vision'. Available online at: http://www.guardian.co.uk/books/2002/oct/12/fiction.benokri/print (accessed 15 November 2010).

Hicks, E. (1991), 'Introduction: border writing as deterritorialization', in E. Hicks, *Border Writing: The Multidimensional Text.* Minneapolis, MN: University of Minnesota Press, pp. xxiii–xxxi.

Highsmith, P. (1999), *The Talented Mr. Ripley.* London: Vintage.

Hoffman, E. (1998), *Lost in Translation.* London: Vintage.

Hutcheon, L. (2006), *A Theory of Adaptation.* New York and London: Routledge.

Iser, W. (1978), *The Act of Reading: A Theory of Aesthetic Response.* Baltimore, MD: Johns Hopkins University.

Kelman, J. (1994), *How Late It Was, How Late.* London: Virago.

Kingsolver, B. (2009), *The Lacuna.* London: Faber and Faber.

Kleffel, R. (2007), 'A conversation with Xiaolu Guo'. Available online at: http://www.bookotron.com/agony/audio/guo_xiaolu_2007.mp3 (accessed 15 November 2010).

Korte, B. (2008), 'Travel Narrative', in Herman et al. (eds) (2008), *Routledge Encyclopedia of Narrative Theory.* London and New York: Routledge, pp. 619–20.

Kreiswirth, M. (2008), 'Narrative turn in the humanities', in D. Herman, M. Jahn and M-L Ryan (eds), *Routledge Encyclopedia of Narrative Theory.* London and New York: Routledge, pp. 377–82.

Kress, G. (2000a), 'Design and transformation: new theories of meaning', in B. Cope and M. Kalantzis (eds), *Multiliteracies: Literacy, Learning and the Design of Social Futures.* New York and London: Routledge, pp. 153–61.

—(2000b), 'Multimodality', in B. Cope and M. Kalantzis (eds), *Multiliteracies: Literacy Learning and the Design of Social Futures.* London and New York: Routledge, pp. 182–202.

—(2003), *Literacy in the New Media Age.* London and New York: Routledge.

Kress, G. and T. van Leeuwen (2001), *Multimodal Discourse: The Modes and Media of Contemporary Communication.* London: Hodder Arnold.

—(2006), *Reading Images: The Grammar of Visual Design* (second edn). Abingdon and New York: Routledge.

Kristeva, J. (1986), 'Word, dialogue and novel', in T. Moi (ed.), *The Kristeva Reader.* Oxford: Basil Blackwell, pp. 34–61.

Lean, D. (1946), *Great Expectations.* Great Britain.

Lejeune, P. (1982), 'The autobiographical contract', in T. Todorov (ed.) *French Literary Theory Today.* Cambridge: Cambridge University, pp. 192–222.

Loffredo, E. and M. Perteghella (2007), *Translation and Creativity: Perspectives on Creative Writing and Translation Studies.* London and New York: Continuum.

Lurie, A. (2007), 'When is a building beautiful?', in *New York Review of Books,* 15 March 2007. Available online at: http://www.nybooks.com/articles/archives/ 2007/mar/15/when-is-a-building-beautiful/ (accessed 5 November 2010).

Lyotard, J-F. (1984), *The Postmodern Condition.* Manchester: Manchester University Press.

Maier, C. (1995), 'Towards a theoretical practice for cross-cultural translation', in A. Dindwaney and C. Maier (eds), *Between Languages and Cultures: Translation and Cross-Cultural Texts.* Pittsburgh, PA and London: University of Pittsburgh Press, pp. 21–38.

Malcolm, I. (1999), 'Writing as an intercultural process', in C. Candlin and K. Hyland (eds), *Writing: Texts, Processes and Practices.* London and New York: Longman, pp. 122–41.

Minghella, A. (2000), *The Talented Mr. Ripley: A Screenplay by Anthony Minghella.* London: Methuen.

Mitchell, K. (2008), *Waves.* London: Oberon Books.

Mitchell, W. (2002), 'Showing seeing: a critique of visual culture'. *Journal of Visual Culture,* 1, 165–81. Available online at: http://vcu.sagepub.com/content/1/2/165 (accessed 15 November 2010).

Ngozi Adichie, C. (2007), *Half of a Yellow Sun.* London: Harper Perennial.

Okri, B. (1992), *The Famished Road.* London: Vintage.

—(2002), *In Arcadia.* London: Weidenfeld and Nicolson.

—(2009), *Tales of Freedom.* London: Rider & Co.

Ovid (2004), *Metamorphoses.* Translated by D. Raeburn. London: Penguin Books.

Page, R. (2007), 'Gender', in D. Herman (ed.), *The Cambridge Companion to Narrative.* Cambridge and New York: Cambridge University Press, pp. 189–202.

—(2008), 'Digital narratives'. Available online at: http://digitalnarratives.blogspot. com/2008_04_01_archive.html (accessed 15 November 2010).

—(2010), 'Introduction', in R. Page (ed.), *New Perspectives on Narrative and Multi-modality.* New York and Abingdon: Routledge, pp. 1–13.

Palmer, J. (2002), 'Ben Okri: great art tries to get us to the place of true enchant-ment'. *The Independent Online.* Available online at: http://www.independent.co. uk/arts-entertainment/books/features/ben-okri-great-art-tries-to-get-us-to-the-place-of-true-enchantment-641793.html (accessed 15 November 2010).

Patel, S. (2009), 'The only place humans can go is to the moon'. Interview with Xiaolu Guo, 25 March 2009. Available online at: http://www.guoxiaolu.com/ REV_WR_dict_Booktin_0309.htm (accessed 15 November 2010).

Pope, R. (2005), *Creativity: Theory, History, Practice.* London and New York: Routledge.

Pullinger, K. and C. Joseph (2005), *Inanimate Alice.* The Bradfield Company Ltd. Available online at: http://www.inanimatealice.com (accessed 15 November 2010).

Pyrhönen, H. (2007), 'Genre', in D. Herman (ed.), *The Cambridge Companion to Narrative.* Cambridge and New York: Cambridge University Press, pp. 109–23.

Readman, M. (2003), *Teaching Scriptwriting, Screenplays and Storyboards for Film and TV Production.* London: BFI Education.

Ricoeur, P. (2000), 'Narrative time', in M. McQuillan (ed.), *The Narrative Reader.* London and New York: Routledge, pp. 255–61.

Rimmon-Kenan, S. (1983), *Narrative Fiction: Contemporary Poetics*. London and New York: Routledge.

Robinson, D. (1997), *Translation and Empire: Postcolonial Theories Explained*. Manchester: St. Jerome Publishing.

Ryan, M-L. (2003), 'On defining narrative media'. *Image and Narrative: Online Magazine of the Visual Narrative*, 6. Available online at: http://www.imageandnarrative. be/inarchive/mediumtheory/marielaureryan.htm (accessed 15 November 2010).

—(2007), 'Towards a definition of narrative', in D. Herman (ed.), *The Cambridge Companion to Narrative*. Cambridge and New York: Cambridge University Press, pp. 22–35.

Sappho (1992), *Poems and Fragments*. Translated by J. Balmer. Newcastle-upon-Tyne: Bloodaxe Books.

Saumarez Smith, C. (2001), 'Another time, another place'. *The Observer*, Sunday, 30 September 2001.

Scott, C. (2000), *Translating Baudelaire*. Exeter: University of Exeter Press.

—(2006), 'Translation and the spaces of reading', in M. Perteghella and E. Loffredo (eds), *Translation and Creativity: Perspectives on Creative Writing and Translation Studies*. London and New York: Continuum, pp. 33–46.

Seawright, P. (2003), *Hidden*. London: The Imperial War Museum.

Sebald, W. G. (2002a), *Austerlitz*. London: Penguin Books.

—(2002b), *The Rings of Saturn*. London: Vintage.

—(2006), *Campo Santo*. London and New York: Penguin Books.

Shevtsova, M. (2006), 'On directing: a conversation with Katie Mitchell'. *New Theatre Quarterly*, 22, (1), 3–18.

Sontag, S. (1977), *On Photography*. London and New York: Penguin Books.

Smith, A. (2007), *Girl Meets Boy*. Edinburgh, New York and Melbourne: Canongate.

Toolan, M. (2001), *Narrative: A Critical Linguistic Introduction* (second edn). London and New York: Routledge.

Trivedi, H. (2007), 'Translating culture and cultural translation', in P. St.-Pierre and P. Kar, *In Translation: Reflections, Refractions, Transformations*. Amsterdam and Philadelphia, PA: John Benjamins Publishing Co., pp. 277–317.

Vaizey, M. (2002), 'Forward', in P. Seawright (2003). *Hidden*. London: The Imperial War Museum.

van Leeuwen, T. (2004), 'Ten reasons why linguists should pay attention to visual communication', in P. Levine and R. Scollon (eds), *Discourse and Technology: Multimodal Discourse Analysis*. Washington, DC: Georgetown University Press, pp. 7–19.

Venuti, L. (1993), 'Translation as cultural politics: regimes of domestication in English'. *Textual Practice*, 2, (2), 208–23.

Vygotsky, L. (1978), *Mind in Society*. Cambridge, MA and London: Harvard University Press.

Warren, J. (2010), 'The progression of digital publishing: innovation and the e-volution of e-books'. *The International Journal of the Book*, 7, (4), 37–53. Champaign, IL: Common Ground Publishing LLC. Available online at: http://www.rand.org/pubs/reprints/2010/RAND_RP1411.pdf (accessed 15 November 2010).

Waters, S. (2006), *The Night Watch*. London: Virago.

Winterson, J. (1995), *Art Objects: Essays on Ecstasy and Effrontery.* London: Jonathan Cape.

—(2001), *Sexing the Cherry.* London: Vintage.

Woolf, V. (1981), *A Room of One's Own.* Orlando, FL: Harcourt Brace Jovanowich.

—(1992a), *The Waves.* London: Penguin Books.

—(1992b), *A Woman's Essays: Selected Essays.* Vol. 1. London: Penguin Books.

—(1993), *Orlando.* London: Virago Press.

Further Reading

In addition to the works cited in the References, the following may be of interest in relation to the ideas presented here.

Brockmeier, J. and D. Carbaugh (eds) (2001), *Narrative and Identity: Studies in Autobiography, Self and Culture*. Amsterdam and Philadephia, PA: John Benjamins.

Currie, M. (2007), *About Time: Narrative, Fiction and the Philosophy of Time*. Edinburgh: Edinburgh University Press.

Gibbons, A. (2010), *Multimodality, Cognition and Experimental Literature*. London and New York: Routledge.

Greaney, M. (2006), *Contemporary Fiction and the Uses of Theory: The Novel from Structuralism to Postmodernism*. Basingstoke, Hampshire: Palgrave Macmillan.

Harper, G. (2010), *On Creative Writing*. Bristol, Buffalo, NY and Toronto: Multilingual Matters.

Herman, D. (2009), *Basic Elements of Narrative*. Oxford: Wiley-Blackwell.

Jiménez-Bellever (2010), 'Speaking in an other's words: coloniality, neo-babelianism, and translation in Guillermo Gómez-Peña's "The New World Border"'. *New Voices in Translation Studies*, 6, 19–35.

Scollon, R. and S. Scollon (2003), *Discourses in Place: Language in the Material World*. London and New York: Routledge.

Index